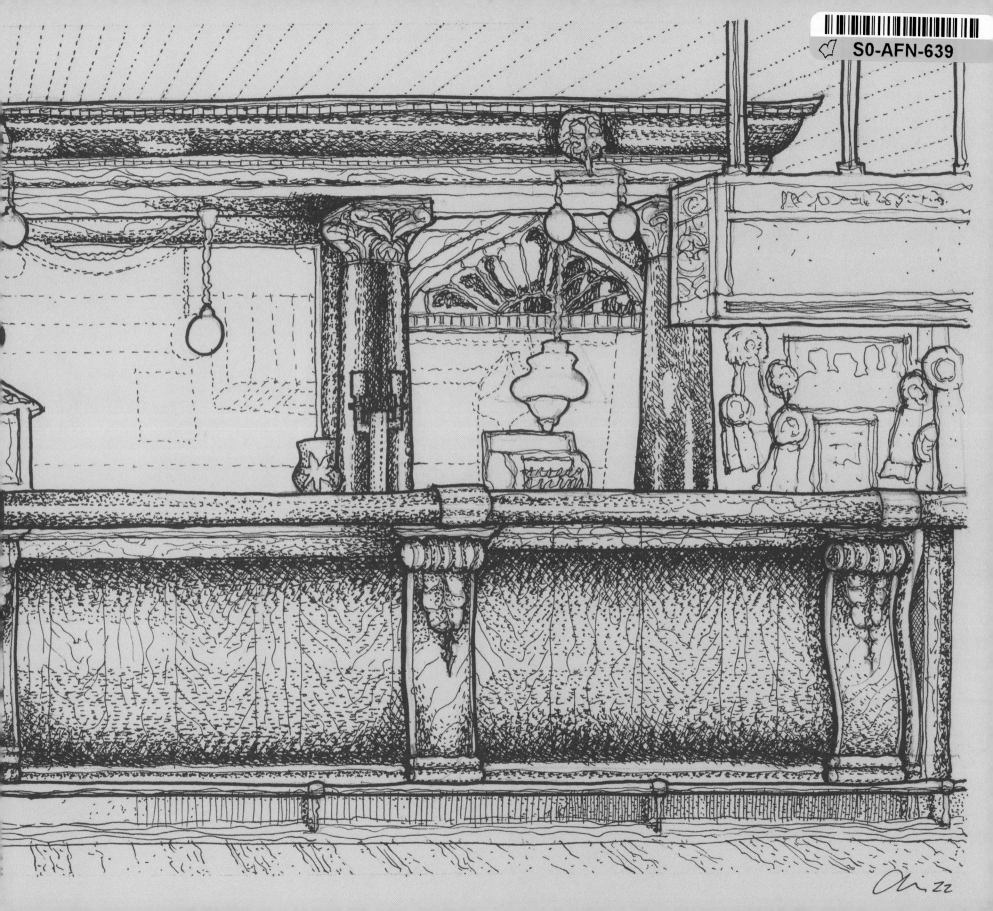

# TOBIN
# JAMES

the book

# TOBIN
# JAMES
## the book

by Claire and Lance Silver
with Tobin James

Recipes by Winery Chef Marc LeDuc
Written by Shawn Forno
Photography by Elaine Silver

CHRONICLE BOOKS
SAN FRANCISCO

ISBN 978-1-7972-1861-8

Manufactured in Canada.

FSC
www.fsc.org

MIX
Paper from
responsible sources
FSC® C016245

Designed by Danielle Youngsmith.
Photography and production by Elaine Silver.
Recipes and food styling by Marc LeDuc.
Text by Shawn Forno.

This book has been set in Circular, League Gothic, and Faith and Glory.

10 9 8 7 6 5 4 3 2 1

Chronicle Books LLC
680 Second Street
San Francisco, CA 94107
www.chroniclebooks.com/custom

To all of you who have sipped and
shared Tobin James wines.

# contents

# welcome

The book in your hands is a loving culmination of thirty-five amazing years at Tobin James Cellars. It's a true testament to how this precious liquid (our wines!) and delicious food can bring family and friends together to celebrate the big milestones and make new memories from simple moments. It's also a celebration of every member of our dedicated Tobin James Cellars team whose energy and care goes into each drop of wine that we make and share with you.

We set out to create this very special Tobin James Cellars "experience" book to share enticing imagery of both our winery home and the exciting dishes that our dynamic chef, Marc LeDuc, creates. We also wanted to share dozens of our favorite "Chef Marc" recipes that pair so perfectly with our stellar wines. But this book is also a reminder to all of our club members, family, friends— our entire growing Tobin James family—that you always have a home here at the winery. We really are one big, happy family!

Through all these years, you have nurtured us, supported us, and watched us grow. We treasured watching our twin daughters grow up at the winery as they helped with events, drying glasses, and playing with Cisco, our dear Australian shepherd and unofficial mascot of Tobin James Cellars. Many of you shared your delicious picnic treats with him and rubbed his belly in the tasting room. You may also remember how he would "belly up to the bar" for a breadstick—or even a little wine! Especially at crush time—Cisco was always great company during our late-night punchdowns when he would enjoy a slice of pizza with the freshly fermenting juice!

We've always loved welcoming you "home" to the winery to taste the latest and greatest of our wines and to catch up on what you've been doing. We also enjoy sharing fun times with you on our cruises and at our epic events, since all of our camaraderie is contagiously FUN! And if you live far away, it's great to chat with you on the phone to let you know all about our wines and for us to hear what's new in your life.

Our amazing Tobin James team gives us every reason to be unendingly grateful. We could not be any prouder of the fine jobs they do and of what caring individuals they are. We are all dedicated to one another and, in turn, all of us at Tobin James are dedicated to you.

Cheers to the next thirty-five years! Let's keep sharing memorable moments with family and friends over delicious food and, of course, our favorite Tobin James wines.

Cheers!

Claire

Claire Silver
co-owner/co-winemaker

ERMIE, TOBY, LANCE, AND CLAIRE
IN THE BARREL ROOM CIRCA 1999

SAME GANG IN 2021,
ONLY GETS BETTER
WITH AGE!

# introduction

You might ask yourself, why a Tobin James cookbook? But is this really a cookbook? Or is it a lifestyle book, perhaps a coffee-table book, or maybe a souvenir book? I hope it becomes all these things to you: a book that you can open to any page and be transported to our tasting room and winery to recall some wonderful memories of past visits. Hopefully, these great recipes will inspire you to get cooking and to drink some Tobin James wines.

## the beginning of a book

Over a decade ago, we had the idea to publish a cookbook with recipes from our first winery chef, Erik. Many of you have met Erik and know what a remarkable chef and person he is. Naiveté ruled, as I thought a chef could just whip out a cookbook with his recipes and flip-phone camera. Nothing much came of that original plan, as it just wasn't a priority at the time. After six wonderful years of Erik's cooking, he decided to move out of the area and take on new responsibilities.

Enter chef Marc LeDuc. For the past ten-plus years, Marc has wowed and delighted our Tobin James family with incredible cuisine for our many parties and other occasions. He is one in a billion, and we are lucky to call him our chef. After the first year of observing his extraordinary talents, I asked him if we could publish a winery cookbook with his recipes. After all, at his previous job, he had written a great cookbook (*The Three Forks Ranch Cookbook*). He agreed. What he didn't say was that creating that book took a team of nine people working on it for quite a long time.

The years went by, and we occasionally asked, "How is the cookbook coming along?" Chef Marc would always respond by telling us that it was coming along just fine, and that he was busy gathering together all of our favorite recipes. Since we had never published a cookbook before, we didn't grasp everything that goes into producing one. It's just recipes and pictures . . . right? Nothing could be further from the truth. So, again, the years went by with no cookbook.

## the book becomes real

One good thing that came from the pandemic was that our daughter Elaine and her boyfriend (now husband), Shawn, came to live with us. They were traveling at the time and got stuck in limbo. Elaine jumped right into winery life and helped us with our wine club, our website, and our social media postings. She immediately became a favorite with everyone at the winery. Shawn is a professional writer who is able to work remotely for his many clients. One night at dinner, Chef Marc brought out his delicious short ribs, and I asked him if he had added the recipe for the ribs to the cookbook. Shawn's eyes lit up, and he asked, "What cookbook?"

Now we had a writer for the book. What about all the beautiful photographs? Elaine, who has long been an avid amateur photographer, equipped herself with some great new gear, and dove headfirst into learning how to photograph food. It's not as simple as setting a plate of food on a table and snapping a photo, which is what, of course, I had thought.

Being stranded in Paso Robles gave Shawn and Elaine a lot of time to work on the cookbook. Months and months of working with Chef Marc finally got us to the point where we knew this book was actually going to happen. But it was far from a finished product.

## making and testing the recipes

One of the most crucial elements of any cookbook is making sure the recipes actually work. Chef Marc has always cooked by feel, and like most chefs, he doesn't write down the recipes he comes up with and then follow them in his day-to-day routine. So, after writing down his recipes, we needed every recipe to be tested by home cooks, following his instructions, to make sure the results would be as tasty as when he prepares them. Who was going to do all this testing?

Enter more family help. We enlisted many of our family and friends, including our trusted staff here at the winery. Everyone on our staff, many of whom you know fondly, grabbed several recipes and took them home to try. Our daughter Melanie volunteered (some might say "coerced" by her twin sister, Elaine) to test the most challenging recipes. Good thing we tested every recipe because several necessary corrections and a number of typos were discovered. Chef Marc's most common error occurred because he is so used to cooking for our events or large groups. When he first handed us his recipe for his famous crab cakes, it called for eighty-five pounds of crabmeat and yielded over eighteen hundred crab cakes. Can you imagine if that recipe had made it into this book? Anyone who tried to follow that recipe would first have had to find a fish market with eighty-five pounds of crabmeat on hand and would then have had to hand over a credit card that could handle the purchase. Needless to say, testing all the recipes for the home cook took months, and again was something that we had never realized was part of creating a cookbook. But we wanted this book to be more than just a cookbook.

## art and design

How do you make a lifestyle book disguise itself as a cookbook? Enter my son-in-law Chris, who is a talented artist and designer. We asked Chris if he could do some of the book layout and contribute a few of his incredible drawings. "Of course I can," he told us, and the final piece of the puzzle was in place.

But wait! We missed something. What did we want on the cover? Arguably, this was the most important piece of the puzzle, as we dreamed of our book gracing countless coffee tables for years to come. We reached out to one of our dearest friends and the most gifted, multi-talented artist we know, Kate Voegele. Kate's talents extend far beyond the canvas, and many of you have been fortunate to have been on one of our cruises where she delighted us with her musical talent. Kate was thrilled that we asked her to create the cover art and immediately began sketching. After just a few tweaks, she started to paint. We hope to have prints of the cover art suitable for framing available in the tasting room, which you can have signed by Kate and any of your favorite staff members.

When I say this book is a family affair, it truly is. Much like our family-owned and -run winery, this book comes from our family and our extended winery family.

Claire and I met Tobin James (Toby) several decades ago, after he had just opened his tasting room. We immediately hit it off and decided to become equal partners in the winery. After a few years, Claire and I took over running the winery and the winemaking duties. As we have grown over the years, we hired a fantastic full-time winemaker in Jeff Poe and have assembled a top-notch cellar team, all of whom have been with us for twenty years or so. But Claire and I still—and always will—do the final blending and have the final say in the winemaking decisions that determine how our delicious wines will ultimately taste when they reach your table.

## welcome to our tasting room

As many of you know, our tasting room is the heart and soul of our winery. We have no marketing department. Nor have we ever hired a public relations firm, as many wineries do. We don't even submit our wines for publication scores. Why? We are so fortunate that we don't have to. Our customers and wine club members help us continue to thrive by recommending us to their friends. Word of mouth has always been how we hope to market our winery, wines, and tasting room. When our customers arrive at the winery, one of the things I often hear our staff say is, "Welcome home!" I also hear, "Welcome to the family," which our staff truly means. When someone signs up for our wine club, they really are joining our family. It's a sincere statement.

## our wine club family

A quick message about our wine club and why it's so special. I know, I know, every winery has a wine club. But we were among the first to start a club, which is now more than twenty-five years old. Claire, Toby, and I packed our first shipment of eighty boxes. Friends and family helped get out the next few shipments, and soon our club had grown to a size where we had to hire staff to assemble the orders. We are now more than thirty thousand members strong, all of whom we consider family. We look at each box as our marketing department, which means every shipment you receive will always exceed your expectations.

## our philosophy

We strive to over-deliver in everything we do, from our parties, our wine club shipments, your experience in our tasting room, and now, this book. But our greatest focus is on producing only the most incredible wines you'll ever drink. We really are proud of them.

This book just had to get into the hands of every one of our family members, so we published enough copies to go into our wine club box. All of our more than thirty thousand wine club members will get a copy. You always share with your family what you love, and for us that means our wine and now this book.

We have been truly blessed to have been able to share a glass of wine with so many of you. Whether it's in our tasting room, at one of our epic parties, or perhaps on one of our unforgettable cruises, every sip of wine we share with you is truly cherished. I hope this book brings you joy and future memories of great food, delicious Tobin James wine, and makes you long for a return trip to "the happiest place on Earth for grown-ups" . . . Tobin James Cellars!

Cheers! And, as always, I hope to see you soon in our tasting room.

*Lance*

Lance Silver
co-owner/co-winemaker

# a letter from Tobin James

It's 1990 and my thirtieth birthday. I'm having dinner with some friends at a swanky Italian restaurant, splurging on some house-made pasta. The place has that vibe—tonight will be filled with great food, fine wine, and good friends.

A buddy of mine gets my attention, then nods his head toward a table to our left. I look over and see an attractive couple holding hands at a candlelit table with a bottle of Tobin James 1987 *Inspiration* Zinfandel. They are smiling and the label is shining in the flickering light. I stare for a minute. I am confused and struggling to understand what I'm seeing. Who are these people? How did that bottle get there? Then it dawns on me that they ordered it from the wine list. I almost faint face-first into my pasta Bolognese.

That wine was my very first vintage, made with my own two hands. This was the first time I'd seen a bottle being enjoyed by people who weren't already friends or hadn't bought it from the trunk of my car. I regained my composure and remembered that, after convincing the restaurant owner that Paso Robles wasn't located in Texas, he had taken a chance by putting the Zin on his list.

This was exciting! I felt proud. I knew that the wine was good, but seeing it on that dinner table put things into an entirely new perspective.

I think we can all agree that wine is one of the finest treats we have in our lives, and food is another. What's magic is they go together so well. Add some family, friends, and fun and you've got a party. From day one at Tobin James, we've told people, "That's not a case of wine. That's twelve different occasions."

We still think that way. We love being part of the good times. God bless America and God bless the James Gang.

Vintage wishes,

Tobin James
co-owner/founding winemaker

# the story

## It all started with six tons of extra grapes.

When a local grape harvester showed up at Eberle Winery with Zinfandel grapes that needed a home, Tobin "Toby" James, a young assistant winemaker, asked if he could have the unwanted grapes to make his own wine.

"Sure, kid, knock yourself out," Gary Eberle replied.

A year and a half later, Toby's first varietal—the now-famous 1987 *Blue Moon* Zinfandel—won double gold medals everywhere it entered. Tobin James Cellars was born.

The Tobin James Cellars tasting room opened at its current location in 1994. Two years later, in 1996, Lance and Claire Silver partnered with Toby to become equal partners and co-winemakers, updating and expanding the winery to become what it is today. Lance and Claire also started the Tobin James "James Gang" Wine Club as a way to share their best and favorite wines with friends and Tobin James Gang wine club members.

What started as one of the first wine clubs in the state has grown steadily over the past twenty-five years into what may be California's largest and most popular wine club. It is also the reason you are all holding this book!

Located eight miles east of Paso Robles on Highway 46, Tobin James Cellars sits on seventy-one acres of vineyards and oak-dotted hills. Built from the ground up on the site of a onetime "10-mile Stagecoach Stop," our old-fashioned Western-style tasting room embraces the rough and rugged frontier history of Paso Robles.

In fact, the first thing you'll see as you stroll into the bustling tasting room is our grand—and recently restored!—1860s Brunswick mahogany bar from Blue Eye, Missouri. Once you've taken it all in, walk right up to it, place your booted foot on its brass rail—just as Jesse James once did—and sample some of our award-winning wines.

Tobin James Cellars is a truly authentic and fun Paso Robles wine-tasting experience. Come visit to find out why "it's all true!"

Stage Coach house - 1953

TOBIN
JAMES
INSPIRATION
1 9 8 9
P A S O   R O B L E S
Z I N F A N D E L

CELLARED AND BOTTLED BY TOBIN JAMES
CELLARS, PASO ROBLES, CALIFORNIA
ALCOHOL 13.8% BY VOLUME

93 9 24

TOBIN JAMES
TASTING ROOM

19

CISCO!

WELCOME HOME!

# thoughts from the chef

When I set out to create this cookbook, I looked back at all the recipes that I've prepared for Tobin James events, parties, cruises, dinners, and the tasting room over the past ten years. Yes, I've been here for over a decade! And honestly, there were a lot of delicious recipes to choose from.

I wanted to showcase dishes that were approachable and made with ingredients that pair beautifully with wine. But most importantly, I wanted recipes that were fun to cook! Some of them are time-tested fan favorites, such as Too Much Garlic & Shrimp Pizza. Others are celebrations of seasonal produce, like our California Heirloom Tomato Gazpacho. But every single recipe is crafted with quality ingredients to pair with our luscious wine.

Each dish is also built around the freshest organic seasonal ingredients—peaches and tomatoes in summer, heavy greens and root vegetables in winter—and locally sourced, grass-fed meats (and butter!). But don't panic if you can't find a specific ingredient in these pages. Use this book as inspiration to create your own dishes to pair with your favorite Tobin James wine.

I want you to have fun with this cookbook. I want you to make a mess. Spill Cabernet on the pages. Get your fingers sticky. This is a wine lover's cookbook. I made these recipes for you, our loyal wine club members. Thank you for always bringing your insatiable appetite for great food, great wine, and a good time to the winery. Go team fun!

Remember that no matter what you're cooking, as long as you spend time in the kitchen with friends or family—or your favorite glass of wine!—you'll get rave reviews.

Raise your glasses and sharpen your knives. (Just be careful out there!)

*Marc*

Marc LeDuc
executive winery chef

# how we pair wine

If you ask the "experts," there are a lot of "rules" you have to follow when you pair wine with your meal: Red wine goes best with red meat. Match white wine with chicken and fish. Unoaked whites go great with citrus. Wine should always be more acidic than food. The list goes on—and on and on.

But here's the secret to pairing food with wine that only true wine enthusiasts know: if you love the food and you love the wine, it's always a perfect pairing.

We designed this cookbook specifically for you—not just people who love wine, but Tobin James "James Gang" wine club members who love our wine. We've talked with you for decades at events and tastings, so we know that everyone enjoys wine in their own personal ways.

You share our wines with the people you love at special occasions or last-minute get-togethers. You save bottles for intimate evenings and sunny days on the patio. And when you pair our wines with moments like that, you can't go wrong.

Lance and Claire have included their personal pairing recommendations for each and every recipe in this cookbook **(see our Wine Pairing Index on page 217),** but if you have a favorite, pop that cork and enjoy! Pair any Tobin James Cellars wine with every recipe in this cookbook, and you'll be in for a perfectly paired meal every time.

We promise.

# bites & appetizers

Smoky Brie crostini, chili-infused watermelon bites, oysters with tarragon butter—if your mouth isn't watering yet, you probably need another glass of wine! At Tobin James, we entertain thousands of guests and wine club members at our parties and events each year, and a huge part of that is knowing how to feed people the bites and appetizers they crave. Stop putting out boring cheese platters. Start your next party or backyard barbecue right with these unique Tobin James bites (that just so happen to pair perfectly with our wines!) for an amazing beginning to any event.

# watermelon, feta, basil & chili bites

**Sweet, salty, and herbaceous, with a surprisingly zesty kick, these easy-to-assemble bites are an inspired twist on a classic summer app-a-teaser.**

1 small, seedless red watermelon, 3 to 4 lb

8 oz feta cheese

1 Tbsp chili powder, plus more if needed

About 1 cup fresh basil or mint leaves

First, remove the rind from the watermelon. To do this, cut a slice off of each end of the watermelon so it will stand upright on a flat end. Then, using a sharp knife, remove the rind and white pulp by slicing downward and following the curve of the melon. You want to remove all the green rind and white pulp.

Cut the red watermelon flesh into 1-inch cubes. Cut the feta into 1-inch cubes, then count the number of cheese cubes. Put the same number of watermelon cubes (see **CHEF PRO TIP**) into a large bowl. Sprinkle the chili powder over all the watermelon cubes, then gently toss the cubes to coat each one on all sides. Add more chili powder if needed to dust each piece lightly.

Once all the cubes are coated to your liking, using appetizer-size wooden skewers, thread a feta cube, a watermelon cube, and a basil leaf onto each skewer for a "garden party" bite that guests will fight over.

**CHEF PRO TIP:** You will have more watermelon cubes than feta cheese cubes. You can serve the extra watermelon cubes in a bowl with toothpicks for spearing or just eat them yourself. Cooking is hard work.

**WINE PAIRING**

*Radiance* **Chardonnay**

*Dream Weaver* **Sparkling**

**PREP TIME**
15 TO 20 MINUTES

**MAKES**
6 TO 8 SERVINGS

**GF/VEG**

# smoky walnut & brie crostini

WINE PAIRING

*Blue Moon
Reserve* Syrah

These go well with just about any wine, but our favorite pairing is the *Blue Moon Reserve* Syrah. Decadent!

1 sourdough baguette

One 8 oz round Brie cheese

¼ cup extra-virgin olive oil

Kosher salt and freshly ground black pepper

6 walnuts in the shell, shelled and halved, or 12 walnut halves

2 Tbsp smoked honey (see **CHEF PRO TIP**)

Preheat the oven to 450°F. Slice twelve ¼-inch-thick slices from the baguette (reserve the rest of the baguette for another use). Slice the Brie into twelve ¼-inch-thick slices, making them the same size as the baguette slices.

Brush a sheet pan with olive oil. Arrange the baguette slices in a single layer on the prepared pan, spacing them evenly apart. Drizzle each slice with 1 teaspoon of the oil and season with salt and pepper.

Place a Brie slice and then a walnut half on each baguette slice and slide the pan into the oven for 1 to 2 minutes. That's just enough time for the cheese to melt a little and the walnut to lightly toast. It's also enough time to pour a glass of wine.

Remove from the oven and drizzle a little of the honey over each crostini. Let the crostini cool before serving. It will be hard to wait, but you don't want to burn your mouth. They can be a little hot out of the oven.

**CHEF PRO TIP:** If you can't find any smoked honey, add 3 drops liquid smoke to 1 cup regular honey. Done!

**PREP TIME**
5 TO 10 MINUTES

**COOK TIME**
1 TO 2 MINUTES

**MAKES**
12 CROSTINI; 4 SERVINGS

**VEG**

WATERMELON, FETA, BASIL & CHILI BITES

SMOKY WALNUT & BRIE CROSTINI

# wild mushroom tartlets

Finally, a mushroom dish for mushroom aficionados and fungi freshmen alike. The crunchy tart shell, earthy mushrooms, rich cream, and acidic vinaigrette bring delightful balance to every bite. Honestly, there's not a lot this dish *doesn't* have!

## WINE PAIRING

*James Gang Reserve* Cabernet Franc

*Big Shot* Rhone Style Blend

**PREP TIME**
20 TO 30 MINUTES

**COOK TIME**
20 TO 25 MINUTES

**MAKES**
6 TO 8 SERVINGS

**VEG**

**MUSHROOM FILLING**

2 Tbsp grapeseed oil

2 Tbsp diced red onion

2 cups roughly chopped wild mushrooms

1 cup walnut halves

Kosher salt and freshly ground black pepper

1 Tbsp unsalted butter, cut into small chunks

**SHERRY CREAM SAUCE**

1 Tbsp diced shallot

½ cup cream sherry

1 cup heavy cream

1 Tbsp thinly sliced chives

Kosher salt and freshly ground black pepper

**SALAD**

½ cup thinly sliced radishes

½ cup finely diced fennel (about 1 bulb)

1 Tbsp extra-virgin olive oil

1 tsp sherry vinegar

Kosher salt and freshly ground black pepper

16 to 20 phyllo cups, each 1 to 2 inches in diameter (see **CHEF PRO TIP**)

Fresh fennel fronds for garnish

**make the mushroom filling**

In a large sauté pan over high heat, warm the oil. Add the onion and sauté until golden brown, 3 to 5 minutes. Add the mushrooms and cook, stirring, until the mushrooms soften, about 2 more minutes.

Transfer the mushrooms and onion to a food processor, add the walnuts, season with salt and pepper, and pulse five or six times to combine. Add the butter and pulse until all the ingredients are evenly incorporated, about 30 seconds. The mixture should have some texture. It should not be a smooth purée. Alternatively, use a chef's knife to chop everything together as finely as you can.

Preheat the oven to 350°F.

**make the sherry cream sauce**

In a small saucepan over medium heat, combine the shallot and sherry, bring to a simmer, and simmer until almost all the sherry evaporates, 3 to 4 minutes. Add the cream, turn down the heat to low, and simmer until slightly reduced, about 10 minutes. Keep an eye on this, as cream sauce likes to boil over and make a mess. Remove from the heat, add the chives, and season with salt and pepper, then cover to keep warm.

**make the salad**

In a small bowl, combine the radishes and fennel and drizzle with the oil and vinegar. Toss to mix, then season with salt and pepper and toss again. Let sit for 5 minutes to allow the vinegar to break down the vegetables a bit.

**make the tartlets**

Fill each phyllo cup three-fourths full with the filling and top with a drizzle of the sauce. The amount of filling and sauce will vary with the size of the tart shells you bought. Place the phyllo cups on a sheet pan. Pop the cups into the oven for about 2 minutes to warm them.

**CHEF PRO TIP:** You can make the phyllo cups from scratch, but perfectly good phyllo cups are sold at well-stocked markets. They're the exact same thing you would make at home.

To assemble and serve, transfer the warm tartlets to a platter and garnish each one with a bit of the salad and a small piece of fennel frond. Get ready for everyone to say they like mushrooms now.

# fig, serrano ham & goat cheese bites

Figs are the nectar of the gods. Now for the salty serrano ham and the creamy goat cheese. Ahhhh. The only thing missing is a glass of *Sundance* Sauvignon Blanc.

8 ripe fresh figs, stemmed

8 tsp fresh goat cheese

4 slices serrano ham, halved lengthwise

Fresh rosemary leaves for garnish

Preheat the oven to 400°F.

Starting at the stem end of a fig, cut an X three-fourths of the way through the fig so it opens like a flower. Don't cut all the way through. Repeat with the remaining figs. Stuff this open cross section in each fig with 1 tsp of the goat cheese.

Wrap a piece of serrano ham around each stuffed fig and secure it with a toothpick. Arrange the figs on a sheet pan.

Bake until the ham starts to brown, 6 to 8 minutes. Do not allow it to burn. Let cool for 5 minutes.

Transfer to a platter and garnish with rosemary. Serve at once. Just make sure your guests don't burn their mouths on the hot cheese!

**WINE PAIRING**

*Sundance* Sauvignon Blanc

*Paradise* Rosé

**PREP TIME**
10 MINUTES

**COOK TIME**
10 MINUTES

**MAKES**
4 SERVINGS

**GF**

AW SHUCKS!

# bbq oysters with spicy tarragon butter

The only thing better than fresh oysters is *smoky* fresh oysters and a nice chilled glass of white wine. We like medium-sized oysters, but just use the freshest you can get.

## WINE PAIRING

*Sundance*
Sauvignon Blanc

*Dream Weaver*
Sparkling

**PREP TIME**
15 TO 20 MINUTES

**COOK TIME**
10 MINUTES

**MAKES**
4 TO 6 SERVINGS

GF

**SPICY TARRAGON BUTTER**

½ cup unsalted butter

1½ Tbsp chopped fresh tarragon, or 2¼ tsp dried tarragon

1 tsp favorite hot sauce

¼ tsp fine sea salt

⅛ tsp freshly ground black pepper

12 oysters

Coarse sea salt or smoked salt for nestling the oysters

Fire up your grill for direct grilling over high heat. Oak and charcoal is a good combination, but a gas grill works, too.

### make the spicy tarragon butter

In a food processor, combine the butter, tarragon, hot sauce, salt, and pepper and pulse six to eight times until blended. Scoop the butter onto the center of a sheet of plastic wrap. Fold a long side of the plastic wrap over the butter, then roll up the butter in the plastic wrap, shaping the butter into a log about 2 inches in diameter. Twist the ends closed, then refrigerate the log until slightly firm, about 15 minutes. When the log is firm, slice it into twelve equal pieces. They'll look like coins.

### grill the oysters

Place the oysters, flat side up, on the grill. Close the grill and cook until the oysters open, 5 to 10 minutes. Transfer to a platter, being careful not to spill any of the oyster liquor from the shells. That's the good stuff.

**CHEF PRO TIP:** If you have an oyster knife, you can take off the top shell before you grill the oysters. Add the butter and grill until the butter is mostly melted. If you don't have an oyster knife, no sweat. Grill 'em up and take off the top once they open as directed. After taking the shell off, add the butter then grill until the butter is melted.

Quickly remove the top shell from each oyster and then loosen the oyster from the bottom shell with an oyster knife if you have one. A butter knife works, too. Top each oyster with a slice of the tarragon butter and return the oysters to the grill to cook until the butter is mostly melted and the oysters are hot, about 1 minute.

Have ready a platter topped with a bed of kosher salt. The salt bed will help keep the oysters from tipping and spilling their liquor. Quickly nestle the oysters in the salt bed. Serve as soon as possible!

# the events

There are events and there are *Tobin James* events.
From the amazing food, the performances by renowned
musicians, and of course, Tobin James wine—once
you go, you know.

Welcome to
the party!

Mediterranean
cruisers

WIND SURF

James Gang Festival

Summer BBQs

FRONT ROW AT TOBIN JAMES

# "one & only" shrimp cocktail

The combination of the pickling spice and the kick from the horseradish adds an extra layer of flavor to even the best-quality shrimp. That duo is put to work in this simple yet enticing appetizer that sets the scene for a great evening. It is a James Gang Festival favorite.

**COCKTAIL SAUCE**

¾ cup chili sauce, such as Heinz Chili Sauce

1 Tbsp fresh lemon juice

1 Tbsp prepared horseradish

**SHRIMP**

2 lemons

½ cup pickling spice

2 Tbsp fine sea salt

12 extra-jumbo shrimp (16/25), peeled with tail on and deveined

**make the cocktail sauce**

In a small bowl, whisk together the chili sauce, lemon juice, and horseradish until well mixed. Cover and chill in the fridge for at least 15 minutes.

**make the shrimp**

Fill a large bowl with ice and water. This will be used to chill the shrimp after they are cooked.

In a large saucepan over high heat, bring 3 qt water to a boil. While the water is heating, cut one of the lemons in half. When the water begins to boil, add the pickling spice, sea salt, and the lemon halves and boil for 5 minutes. Strain the seasoned water through a fine-mesh sieve and return it to the pan.

Bring the seasoned water back to a boil over high heat and add the shrimp. Turn down the heat to medium and simmer until the shrimp are cooked through, for 5 to 8 minutes.

Once the shrimp are ready, drain them and add them to the bowl of ice water. Chill for 10 minutes. While you are waiting for them to chill, cut the remaining lemon into wedges and serve everyone a glass of chilled white wine.

Drain the shrimp and pat dry. Thread the shrimp on to twelve appetizer-size wooden skewers or wooden cocktail forks. Arrange the skewers on a platter with the sauce dolloped on each shrimp.

**WINE PAIRING**

*Sundance* Sauvignon Blanc

*James Gang Reserve* Chardonnay

*Paradise* Rosé

**PREP TIME**
20 MINUTES

**COOK TIME**
15 TO 20 MINUTES

**MAKES**
4 TO 6 SERVINGS

**GF**

THE PARTY HAS STARTED!

# ahi tuna poke

These poke bites are a another James Gang Festival favorite. Get the freshest tuna you can, deep-fry those wontons, and it's "one bite, good night." You'll see.

**PREP TIME**
20 TO 25 MINUTES

**COOK TIME**
15 MINUTES

**MAKES**
6 TO 8 SERVINGS

## POKE

1 lb ahi (yellowfin) tuna (grade #1—aka sushi or sashimi grade—preferred)

3 green onions, white and green parts, sliced

2 Tbsp tamari or soy sauce

1 Tbsp toasted sesame oil or sesame chili oil (for extra spice)

1 Tbsp mixed black and white sesame seeds

Freshly ground black pepper

## WONTON WRAPPERS

Grapeseed oil for deep-frying

10 square wonton wrappers

1 green onion, green and white parts, sliced for garnish

### make the poke

Trim away any bloodlines, skin, and visible sinew from the tuna. Cut the tuna into ½-inch cubes. In a medium glass or stainless-steel bowl, combine the tuna, green onions, tamari, sesame oil, sesame seeds, and a few grinds of pepper and toss to mix evenly. Cover and chill for 15 to 20 minutes. While the poke is chilling, fry the wonton wrappers.

### fry the wonton wrappers

Pour the grapeseed oil to a depth of 2 to 3 inches into a medium, heavy saucepan, making sure it is not more than half full. Heat the oil to 350°F on a deep-frying thermometer. This should take around 10 minutes, but every stove is different. It's important to get the temperature exactly right, so pay close attention.

While the oil is heating, cut each wonton wrapper in half on the diagonal to make two triangles. Line a sheet pan with paper towels and set it near the stove.

Working in batches of four or five triangles, add the wonton wrappers to the hot oil, making sure they don't fold up as they fry. Cook until crispy and golden brown, 2 to 3 minutes. Using a slotted spoon, transfer them to the towel-lined sheet pan to drain. Repeat until all the wrappers are fried, then let cool to room temperature.

To serve, top each wonton triangle with a spoonful of the tuna mixture and arrange on a platter. Garnish with the green onion and serve with glasses of sparkling *Dream Weaver*.

# dungeness crab cakes

Here's a playful twist on the classic Maryland crab cake. Enjoy the pop of creamy goodness from the cream cheese that pairs surprisingly well with a full-bodied white wine, like our *James Gang Reserve* Chardonnay.

**PREP TIME**
15 MINUTES (PLUS 1 HOUR TO CHILL)

**COOK TIME**
15 MINUTES

**MAKES**
6 TO 8 CRAB CAKES

1 lb fresh Dungeness crabmeat

4 to 6 Tbsp grapeseed oil

½ cup diced celery

½ cup diced sweet yellow onion

⅓ cup mayonnaise

1 egg

2 Tbsp fresh lemon juice

1 Tbsp yellow mustard

½ cup panko bread crumbs

1 tsp Old Bay Seasoning

¼ cup chopped fresh flat-leaf parsley

4 oz cream cheese, cut into ¼-inch chunks

1 cup Tartar Sauce (page 208) or cocktail sauce (page 38)

First, pick through the crabmeat to make sure no bits of shell or cartilage are hidden.

---

**CHEF PRO TIP:** As you pick through the crabmeat, try to keep the meat in as many big chunks as possible. The crab cakes will look (and taste) better!

---

In a small frying pan over medium heat, warm 2 Tbsp of the oil. Add the celery and onion and cook, stirring occasionally, until they start to soften, about 2 minutes. You want them still to have a little crunch. Add them to a medium bowl and let cool for 5 minutes.

Add the mayonnaise, egg, lemon juice, mustard, bread crumbs, Old Bay Seasoning, and parsley to the bowl with the celery and onion and whisk together until all the ingredients are evenly distributed. Gently fold in the crabmeat. Be careful not to overmix, as you want to see crab chunks in the mixture.

Adding about five pieces at a time, gently mix the cream cheese chunks into the crab mixture. Make sure they are dispersed evenly throughout the mixture. Cover and chill for 1 hour before cooking.

Preheat the oven to 400°F.

Using a 2½- to 3-inch ring mold or your hands, shape the crab cakes about 1 inch thick. If you're using a ring mold, gently press the crab mixture down into the mold with a spoon. This light pressure will help the cakes to hold together during cooking. As each cake is shaped, set it aside on a sheet pan.

Coat a sheet pan with cooking spray and set it near the stove. Add enough of the grapeseed oil (about 2 Tbsp) to a large cast-iron frying pan to cover the bottom and place the pan over medium heat. When the oil begins to smoke lightly, add three or four of the crab cakes, being careful not to crowd the pan, and cook, turning once, until nicely browned on both sides, about 2 minutes on each side. Transfer the cakes to the prepared sheet pan. Repeat with the remaining crab cakes, adding more oil to the pan as needed.

When all the crab cakes are browned, slide the sheet pan into the oven and bake the cakes until they are heated through, 6 to 8 minutes. Serve at once with the sauce of your choice and a delicious glass of *James Gang Reserve* Chardonnay.

LANCE'S FAVORITE!

# brie crostini with bacon-onion marmalade

**Sweet. Salty. Rich. Creamy. This dish is well balanced and delicious, just like a good bottle of Zinfandel.**

1 French-style baguette

Extra-virgin olive oil, for brushing

Kosher salt and freshly ground black pepper

One 6-oz round Brie cheese

¾ cup Bacon-Onion Marmalade (page 209)

Preheat the oven to 450°F. Slice the baguette into ¼-inch-thick slices. Arrange the slices on a large sheet pan, brush each slice on both sides with olive oil, and then season the top with salt and pepper. Place in the oven and bake, turning once, until lightly toasted on both sides, about 4 minutes total.

To assemble the crostini, slice the Brie into ¼-inch-thick slices, making them about the same size as the baguette slices. Set a piece of Brie on each toasted baguette slice and top with a dollop (about ½ oz) of the bacon marmalade. *Voilà*.

## WINE PAIRING

*Ballistic Zinfandel*

*James Gang Reserve Zinfandel*

*French Camp Vineyard Zinfandel*

**PREP TIME**
5 TO 10 MINUTES

**COOK TIME**
10 MINUTES (PLUS 30 MINUTES FOR THE "MARMALADE")

**MAKES**
6 TO 8 SERVINGS

# low 'n' slow tri-tip with red wine aioli

Tri-tip is packed with lean, beefy flavor. When you cook it "low and slow" and pair it with a creamy aioli (and a nice bottle of red), it's simply irresistible for your next barbecue.

## TRI-TIP

1 whole tri-tip (1½ to 2 lb), trimmed of excess fat and silverskin

Kosher salt and freshly ground black pepper

## RED WINE AIOLI

1½ cups *Notorious* **Cabernet Sauvignon**

4 garlic cloves, minced

½ cup mayonnaise

½ cup full-fat plain yogurt

Pinch of cayenne pepper

Kosher salt and freshly ground black pepper

Crusty bread, for serving

### grill the tri-tip

Season the tri-tip generously with salt and pepper, then let the meat come to room temperature for about 30 minutes.

While that's happening, fire up the grill. Gas, wood, or charcoal all work great. Set up two zones, one for direct grilling over high heat and one for indirect grilling over no heat.

Once the meat is ready to cook, put it on the cooking grate directly over the hottest part of the fire and sear it on all sides—top, bottom, and every side—until nice and brown, 10 to 15 minutes total.

---

**CHEF PRO TIP:** Tri-tip is usually a relatively tough cut of meat. That's why I suggest cooking tri-tip to medium instead of medium-rare. The extra cook—at low temperature—will help break down the meat to make it more tender and delicious.

---

After the meat is seared and browned, move it to the area of the grill set up for indirect heat. You don't want the meat over the direct flames right now. The optimal grill temperature is between 200°F and 250°F. Once it is on the cooler area, close the lid. This will trap the heat and help cook the meat from all sides like an oven. If your grill doesn't have a lid, flip the meat over every 15 to 20 minutes.

The goal is to cook the meat low and slow—ideally for 2 to 3 hours (or more) if your grill heat is low enough. Check the internal temperature of the meat with an instant-read thermometer every 30 minutes until it reaches 130°F. Once it reaches 130°F, check it every 15 minutes until it reaches 135°F.

Take the meat off the grill and let it rest on a cutting board for 10 minutes before slicing. You should end up with a light pink center. If you prefer your tri-tip medium-rare, take it off at 130°F.

### make the red wine aioli

You can make this simple (but delicious) sauce while the meat is grilling. In a medium saucepan over medium heat, combine the wine and garlic, bring to a simmer, and simmer until reduced to ½ cup, 10 to 15 minutes. Remove from the heat, let cool, transfer to a medium glass or stainless-steel bowl, cover, and refrigerate until cold, about 10 minutes.

Add the mayonnaise, yogurt, and cayenne to the cold reduced wine and whisk until blended. Season with a little salt and black pepper. Cover and refrigerate until serving.

For serving, we like to cut the tri-tip against the grain into thin slices. Accompany it with the aioli and slices of crusty bread. Don't forget to pour everyone a glass of red to go with this rich, robust, red-blooded snack.

## WINE PAIRING

*Notorious* **Cabernet Sauvignon** (for a perfect pairing)

*James Gang Reserve* **Petit Verdot**

*Palindrome* **Tannat**

**PREP TIME**
30 MINUTES

**COOK TIME**
2 TO 3 HOURS

**MAKES**
6 TO 8 SERVINGS

**GF**

ONE OF TOBY'S FAVORITES!

# flank steak bites

If you've ever visited the tasting room at Tobin James, this appetizer needs no introduction. It is the hands-down fan favorite. Bring the taste of Paso to your next party with these lightly grilled, juicy, beefy bites.

## WINE PAIRING

All your favorite Tobin James red wines

**PREP TIME**
10 TO 15 MINUTES

**COOK TIME**
15 TO 20 MINUTES

**MAKES**
6 TO 8 SERVINGS

## SAUCE

1 cup mayonnaise

½ cup sour cream

1 tsp tomato paste

1 tsp fresh lemon juice

1 tsp honey

½ tsp Worcestershire sauce

1 tsp mustard powder

1 tsp onion powder

1 tsp garlic powder

2 drops liquid smoke

## STEAK

1 flank steak, 1½ to 2 lb

3 Tbsp Montreal steak seasoning

Grapeseed oil, for brushing

### make the sauce

In a medium glass or stainless-steel bowl, whisk together the mayonnaise, sour cream, tomato paste, lemon juice, honey, Worcestershire sauce, mustard powder, onion powder, garlic powder, and liquid smoke until thoroughly blended. When your forearm starts cramping, you're good. Cover and chill while you cook the steak.

### make the flank steak

Fire up the grill for direct grilling over high heat. Pull the flank out of the refrigerator 10 minutes before cooking. Generously season both sides with the Montreal seasoning.

Lightly brush the cooking grate with grapeseed oil to prevent the meat from sticking. Or dip a kitchen towel in grapeseed oil and rub the oil on the grate. Set a wire rack on a sheet pan and place it near the grill.

Cook the steak, turning once, for 5 to 8 minutes on each side; the timing depends on your desired doneness. For medium-rare, cook the steak for about 10 minutes total; for medium, cook the steak about 16 minutes. Transfer the meat to the rack and let it rest until it stops dripping, 5 to 10 minutes.

**CHEF PRO TIP:** You can let the meat rest on a plate, but a rack is better because it allows air to circulate around the meat, cooling it evenly, instead of trapping the heat underneath.

When the steak has rested, cut into 1-inch cubes. Drizzle each cube with a little of the sauce and spear the cube with a toothpick. Then make sure you have one hand free for high fives.

salads

Pairing wine with salad has always been a challenge. Vinaigrettes are often harsh on the palate, which is why we created each of the salads in this chapter to be less acidic, more earthy, and packed with rich yet balanced flavors. You can confidently pair them with your favorite Tobin James wines. Earthy mushrooms. Herbaceous greens. Grilled leaves exuding smoke, char, and a flush of heat. The right salad can set the tone of the meal. So kick-start your next dinner with any of these nine salads to add a rich blend of tastes and textures that will tease the aromas and tasting notes from whichever Tobin James wine you choose.

# french bibb lettuce & herbs

**WINE PAIRING**

*Paradise* Rosé

Buttery Bibb lettuce leaves and a classic vinaigrette are sometimes all you need for a great salad. Add (a few) glasses of *Paradise* Rosé and you've got yourself a great French-style salad that's perfect for a spring or summer lunch outdoors! Here's how to make an almost-too-simple salad that still packs a wallop of flavor in every bite.

**PREP TIME**
15 TO 20 MINUTES

**MAKES**
4 SERVINGS

**GF/VEG/VG**

**MUSTARD VINAIGRETTE**

1 Tbsp Dijon mustard

¼ cup red wine vinegar

1 cup extra-virgin olive oil

Kosher salt and freshly ground black pepper

**SALAD**

4 small heads Bibb lettuce (1 head per serving)

Kosher salt and freshly ground black pepper

6 tsp minced shallot

6 tsp minced fresh chives

4 Tbsp fresh flat-leaf parsley leaves

4 Tbsp fresh tarragon leaves

4 Tbsp fresh chervil leaves

4 tsp fresh lemon juice

**make the mustard vinaigrette**

In a small mason jar, combine the mustard, vinegar, and oil and season with salt and pepper. Screw on the lid and shake the jar like a Polaroid picture. (If you prefer your vinaigrette less tart, add an additional ½ cup oil.) Set aside while you prep the salad. You will need only about ⅔ cup vinaigrette for this recipe. Refrigerate the remaining vinaigrette for up to 5 days and use for other salads.

**make the salad**

Carefully cut out the core from each head of lettuce and separate the leaves (you can toss out any damaged or tough outer leaves). Make sure you keep each head of lettuce together, as you need to reassemble the heads for each individual salad. The easiest way to do that is to work with one head at a time.

**CHEF PRO TIP:** Discard the first two layers of leaves from each head (but that's just one chef's opinion).

Once you've prepped all the Bibb lettuce heads, fill a large bowl with cold water and immerse the leaves from one head in the water to refresh them and to remove any dirt. Then lift them out of the water, spin dry in a salad spinner, and set aside. Repeat with the remaining heads, one at a time.

Next, place the leaves from a single head of lettuce in a medium bowl. Sprinkle with a pinch of salt, a few grinds of pepper, 1½ tsp each of the shallot and chives, and 1 Tbsp each of the parsley, tarragon, and chervil. Drizzle with 2 Tbsp of the vinaigrette and 1 tsp of the lemon juice and toss to coat evenly. Remove the outer leaves from the bowl, arrange them as a base on an individual serving plate, then, using the remaining leaves in the bowl, rebuild the head of lettuce on the plate, ending with the smallest, most tender leaves. Repeat with the remaining heads of lettuce to build three more salads the same way.

Drizzle a little more vinaigrette on each plate for presentation, then open a bottle of *Paradise* Rosé to celebrate your edible and luscious masterpiece!

A CLAIRE FAVORITE. SHE LOVES KALE...AND MASSAGES

# sea salt–massaged kale salad

This bright, crisp salad is what happens when you take simple, fresh ingredients and pamper them a little bit. But don't panic if you've never "massaged" your salad before. It's easier than it sounds. Just grab the greens and give them a good rubdown with olive oil and sea salt. Massaging the kale softens up some of the tougher edges and coarse leaves for a tender, more sophisticated salad. You don't need reservations at a fancy spa to treat yourself. Once you've tasted the subtle crunch of Sea Salt–Massaged Kale Salad with a glass of *Sundance* Sauvignon Blanc or even a glass of *Primo* Sangiovese, you'll know the true meaning of bliss.

**WINE PAIRING**

*Sundance*
Sauvignon Blanc

*Primo*
Sangiovese

**PREP TIME**
15 TO 20 MINUTES

**MAKES**
4 SERVINGS

**GF/VEG**

**RED WINE VINAIGRETTE**

1½ Tbsp Dijon mustard

½ cup red wine vinegar

½ tsp honey

1 cup extra-virgin olive oil

Fine sea salt and freshly ground black pepper

**SALAD**

4 cups finely chopped Lacinato kale

Extra-virgin olive oil for drizzling

Fine sea salt and freshly ground black pepper

1 cup finely chopped red cabbage

¼ cup Pickled Red Onions (page 211)

¾ cup diced tomato

¾ cup diced radishes

½ cup diced English cucumber

Dijon mustard for serving

**make the red wine vinaigrette**

In a small bowl, whisk together the mustard, vinegar, and honey. Then slowly whisk in the oil. Season with salt and pepper. That's it. (If you prefer your vinaigrette less tart, add an additional ½ cup oil.)

**make the salad**

Put the kale into a medium bowl. Drizzle with a little oil, sprinkle with a small pinch of sea salt, and massage the kale for about 30 seconds. You don't want to overdo it. You'll know you're finished when the kale starts to look a little darker (and more relaxed!).

**CHEF PRO TIP:** "Massaging" a salad is one of the best ways to soften up tough greens (like kale), which makes them easier to eat, easier to digest, and better at soaking up your delicious dressing. Your jaw will thank you.

Add the cabbage, pickled onions, tomato, radishes, and cucumber and toss with as much dressing as you like. Season with salt and pepper.

For that extra gourmet presentation, add a smear of Dijon mustard to each salad plate, then arrange the salad on top and serve.

# melon & arugula salad

This salad is almost deceptively simple. Honestly, it's mostly just fresh arugula and melon slices with a clean, crisp tarragon vinaigrette. But when the round sweetness of the melon and the sharp acidity and earthy finish of the radishes and tarragon vinaigrette come together, the result is a seesaw of contrasting flavors. If you don't want to put your finger on just one side of the flavor scale, the salad goes equally well with an off-dry *James Gang Reserve* Riesling or a dry *Sundance* Sauvignon Blanc.

**WINE PAIRING**

*Sundance* **Sauvignon Blanc**

*James Gang Reserve* **Riesling**

---

**PREP TIME**
30 TO 40 MINUTES

**MAKES**
4 SERVINGS

**GF/VEG/VG**

## TARRAGON VINAIGRETTE

2 Tbsp sherry vinegar

1 Tbsp minced shallot

1 tsp Dijon mustard

1 Tbsp chopped fresh tarragon leaves

6 Tbsp extra-virgin olive oil

Kosher salt and freshly ground black pepper

## SALAD

8 cups arugula

1 cup microgreens, such as micro arugula

½ cup loosely packed fresh tarragon leaves

2 cups heirloom cherry tomatoes, halved

4 radishes, thinly sliced

12 thin slices Canary melon, skinned and seeded (see **CHEF PRO TIP**)

### make the tarragon vinaigrette

Put the vinegar and shallot into a small mason jar and let sit for 30 minutes. Then add the mustard, tarragon, and oil and season with salt and pepper. Screw on the lid and shake the jar like a boss for about 30 seconds. Just pretend you're Tom Cruise making a cocktail and you'll be fine. (You will have vinaigrette left over. Store it in an airtight container in the refrigerator for up to 5 days and use it however you like.)

---

**CHEF PRO TIP:** If you cannot find a Canary melon, a Crenshaw melon will work just as well. If you can't find either of them, just use your favorite melon.

---

### make the salad

In a large bowl, combine the arugula, micro-greens, tarragon, and all but a few of the tomato halves and radish slices. Add 2 Tbsp of the vinaigrette and toss it all together. If you make a mess, pour yourself a glass of *Sundance* **Sauvignon Blanc** and remember that it's just a salad. You're gonna be okay.

Divide the tossed salad among four salad plates. Divide and arrange the melon slices next to the salads on each plate. Top the melon slices with the reserved tomatoes and radish slices for that extra fancy touch. Drizzle the melon with dressing. Cheers!

CANARY MELON

CRENSHAW MELON

# the tasting room

Welcome home.

Our grand antique bar, circa 1994.

BELLY UP!

# salt-roasted beet & arugula salad

This dish is all about textures and intense flavors. The snappy spice of fresh arugula blends with the meatiness of the beets and light acidity of the oranges. Topped with creamy goat cheese and crunchy almonds, this dish is a feast for the senses. Roasting beets in salt is not for the faint of heart. But it's a great way to concentrate the rich, earthy flavors of the beets for a salad unlike anything you've ever tried. And the good news is that you can open a bottle of *Sundance* Sauvignon Blanc while you wait for the beets to roast.

**WINE PAIRING**

*Sundance*
Sauvignon Blanc

**PREP TIME**
10 TO 15 MINUTES

**COOK TIME**
1 HOUR (FOR
ROASTING BEETS)

**MAKES**
4 SERVINGS

**GF/VEG**

Salt-Roasted Beets
(page 203)

**ORANGE VINAIGRETTE**

½ cup fresh orange juice

¼ cup white wine vinegar

1 Tbsp stone-ground mustard

¾ cup extra-virgin olive oil

Kosher salt and freshly ground black pepper

**SALAD**

4 oranges

6 cups arugula (about 5 oz)

2 carrots, peeled and shaved lengthwise into ribbons

½ cup sliced almonds, lightly toasted

4 oz fresh goat cheese

### make the salt-roasted beets

Roast the beets as directed, then let cool and peel as directed. Thinly slice the beets or cut them into six to eight wedges.

### make the vinaigrette

While the beets are roasting, make the vinaigrette. In a blender, combine the orange juice, vinegar, and mustard and pulse several times to mix. With the blender running on medium speed, slowly add the oil and blend until the mixture emulsifies. If the vinaigrette is too thick, thin it with a little water and blend briefly to mix. Turn off the blender, season the vinaigrette with salt and pepper, and set aside.

### make the salad

Cut a slice off the top and bottom of an orange to expose the flesh, then stand the orange upright. Using a sharp knife, and following the contour of the fruit, cut downward to slice off the peel and pith in wide slices. Slice the peeled orange into round segments about ¼ inch thick. Remove the seeds as needed. Repeat with the remaining oranges.

In a large bowl, toss the arugula and carrots with 3 Tbsp of the vinaigrette. Divide the salad among four salad plates. Garnish the salads with the beets, orange segments, and almonds, dividing them evenly, and finish each salad with a dollop of the goat cheese. You'll have some dressing left over. Store it in a covered container in the fridge for up to 5 days and use it for whatever you want. You're the chef, so have fun with it.

# "char-donnay" grilled romaine salad

Any wine lover will tell you that it's tough to pair a salad with wine. Because it is. That's what makes this wine-friendly salad so special. The touch of smokiness from grilling the romaine gives this salad the extra oomph it needs to pair beautifully with our crisp *James Gang Reserve* Chardonnay, which we age in a combination of light- and medium-charred French oak barrels. A char-grilled romaine salad is also a perfect addition to a hearty BBQ spread, especially since you're firing up the grill anyway!

**DRESSING**

2 Tbsp unsalted butter

6 cups thinly sliced yellow onions (about 3 medium onions)

Kosher salt and freshly ground black pepper

1 Tbsp Dijon mustard

3 Tbsp sherry vinegar

2 Tbsp soy sauce or tamari

7 Tbsp extra-virgin olive oil

**SALAD**

2 heads romaine lettuce

Grapeseed oil for brushing

Kosher salt and freshly ground black pepper

1 cup thinly sliced or julienned radishes

16 cherry tomatoes, halved

1 crisp green apple, cored, peeled, and cut into ¼-inch cubes

½ cup fresh micro chervil or fresh dill fronds

**make the dressing**

Start by caramelizing the onions. In a large cast-iron frying pan over medium heat, melt the butter. Add the onions and stir them gently to coat with the butter. Cook the onions, checking on them often and stirring to prevent scorching, until golden brown and delicious, about 20 minutes. Season with salt and pepper.

Put 1 cup of the caramelized onions in a blender and reserve the remainder for garnish. Add the mustard, vinegar, soy sauce, 3 Tbsp water, and ⅛ tsp pepper and blend on high speed until smooth, about 1 minute. With the blender running on low speed, slowly add the olive oil and blend until the mixture emulsifies. If the vinaigrette is too thick, thin it with a little water and blend briefly to mix. Transfer to a covered container and chill for at least 10 minutes before using.

**make the salad**

Next, fire up the grill for direct grilling over high heat (or heat a cast-iron grill pan over high heat on the stove top). Remove any

wilted outer leaves from the romaine heads, then cut each head in half lengthwise. Brush the cut side of each half with grapeseed oil and season lightly with salt and pepper. Grill the romaine, cut side down, until just lightly charred, 30 to 60 seconds.

---

**CHEF PRO TIP:** The leaves char quickly, so keep an eye on them. You want only a light char on the outside. You're not trying to "cook" the lettuce. Each half should still be cold in the center.

---

Place a romaine half, cut side up, on each salad plate. Dress the halves with as much dressing as you like and garnish with the reserved caramelized onions, the radishes, tomatoes, and apple, dividing them evenly. Finish with some micro chervil and serve.

Toast your grill-master skills with a nice chilled glass of *James Gang Reserve* Chardonnay. You've earned it!

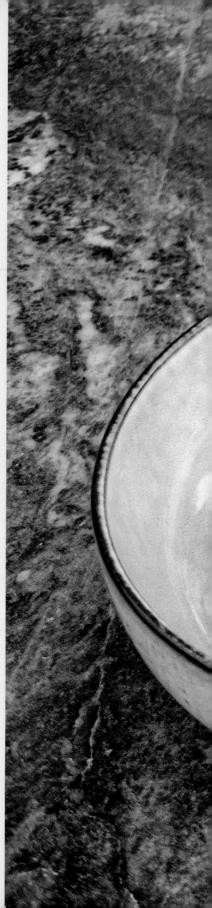

A PERFECT CHAR

WINE PAIRING

*James Gang Reserve* **Chardonnay**

**PREP TIME**
15 TO 20 MINUTES

**COOK TIME**
25 MINUTES

**MAKES**
4 SERVINGS

**GF/VEG**

# greek salad bites

This might be the most sophisticated salad that you can eat with your hands. No, really. Grab these lettuce cups like a taco and dive in. No silverware required! The crunch of fresh vegetables pairs perfectly with the soft Bibb lettuce cups for a welcoming and enticing mouthfeel that screams for a chilled bottle of your favorite white wine, like our *Sundance* Sauvignon Blanc, or even our famous *Paradise* Rosé. It's time to get your hands messy in the most delicious way possible. Here's how to make a one-of-a-kind Greek salad.

**WINE PAIRING**

*Sundance*
Sauvignon Blanc

*Paradise* Rosé

**PREP TIME**
30 TO 45 MINUTES

**MAKES**
4 TO 6 SERVINGS

**GF/VEG**

## GREEK DRESSING

¼ tsp minced garlic cloves

½ tsp dried basil leaves

¼ tsp chopped fresh oregano leaves

1½ tsp Dijon mustard

5 Tbsp red wine vinegar

2 Tbsp fresh lemon juice

½ tsp sugar

½ cup extra-virgin olive oil

Kosher salt (optional)

## SALAD

2 heads Bibb lettuce

2 cups diced heirloom tomatoes, in ⅓-inch dice

1 cup diced English cucumber, in ⅓-inch dice

1 cup seeded and diced red bell peppers, in ⅓-inch dice

1 cup diced feta cheese, in ⅓-inch dice

¼ cup Castelvetrano olives, pitted and halved

¼ cup Kalamata olives, pitted and halved

¼ cup sliced peperoncinis

1 Tbsp chopped fresh dill

Kosher salt and freshly ground black pepper

1 cup Pickled Red Onions (page 211), optional

## make the greek dressing

In a small mason jar, combine the garlic, basil, oregano, mustard, vinegar, lemon juice, sugar, and oil. Screw on the lid and shake the jar vigorously until well mixed, about 30 seconds. Taste and add a little salt if you like, keeping in mind the feta and olives will add salt to the finished salad. Refrigerate for at least 15 minutes before using.

If you want an even creamier dressing, put all the ingredients except the oil into a blender and pulse several times to mix. With the blender running on high speed, slowly add the oil and blend until the mixture emulsifies and is creamy. Transfer to a covered container and refrigerate for at least 15 minutes before using.

**CHEF PRO TIP:** The point of using a blender to make the dressing is to "emulsify" the mixture. Adding air by blending gives the dressing a luxurious mouthfeel. To be clear, this is an extra step. You don't need a blender to make a delicious Greek salad dressing. But if you like creamy dressing, the extra effort is worth it.

## make the salad

Trim away the core from the lettuce heads and separate and wash the leaves. You need three good leaves for each serving.

In a medium bowl, combine the tomatoes, cucumber, bell peppers, feta cheese, Castelvetrano and Kalamata olives, peperoncinis, and dill. Drizzle the dressing over the top and season with salt and pepper. Mix with a large spoon to coat the salad evenly with the dressing.

Place the lettuce leaves on a large serving plate and pile each leaf cup high with a spoonful of the salad mixture. If using pickled onions, add them for a final touch. Serve with a glass of chilled *Paradise* Rosé.

# kale, caesar!

We love using kale for this Caesar salad instead of the more traditional romaine because of the extra crunch and richer, earthier notes. Topped with a creamy cashew dressing (no egg yolk here!) and finished with a hint of lemon zest, this fresh take on an old classic will make you rethink what a Caesar salad should be. And if you omit the pecorino romano, this salad is vegan. If you can, serve it during heirloom tomato season (summer and early fall) with thick slices of ripe tomatoes for a balanced vegan-friendly dish that pairs spectacularly with a chilled glass of *Radiance* Chardonnay or our dry *Sundance* Sauvignon Blanc.

## WINE PAIRING

*Sundance*
Sauvignon Blanc

*Radiance*
Chardonnay

**PREP TIME**
15 TO 20 MINUTES

**MAKES**
4 SERVINGS

GF/VEG/VG

## CAESAR DRESSING

¼ cup raw cashews

3 Tbsp chopped garlic

2 tsp drained capers

1 tsp Dijon mustard

2 Tbsp fresh lemon juice

½ tsp finely grated lemon zest

2 Tbsp extra-virgin olive oil

¼ tsp fine sea salt

Freshly ground black pepper

## SALAD

2 heads Lacinato kale, stemmed

Extra-virgin olive oil, for drizzling

Pinch of fine sea salt

2 heirloom tomatoes, sliced

1 cup thinly sliced radishes

1 cup shaved or grated pecorino romano or Parmesan cheese

Freshly ground black pepper

### make the caesar dressing

In a small bowl, soak the cashews in ¼ cup water for 15 minutes. Add the soaked cashews and the soaking water to a blender and blend on high speed until smooth, about 30 seconds. The mixture should be the consistency of honey. You may need to add more water, depending on the size of the cashews.

Add the garlic, capers, mustard, lemon juice, and lemon zest and pulse several times to mix. With the blender running on low speed, slowly add the oil and blend until the mixture emulsifies. Once all the oil is added, you can add more water if you want a thinner dressing. Pour the dressing into a bowl and season with the salt and a grind or two of pepper.

### make the salad

Chiffonade the kale.

---

**CHEF PRO TIP:** The word *chiffonade* means "little ribbons" in French. The best way to chiffonade kale is to stack the leaves, roll up the stack lengthwise into a tight cylinder (like a cigar), and slice very thinly crosswise with a sharp knife. You'll end up with long, narrow ribbons and a sense of accomplishment.

---

Put the kale into a large bowl. Drizzle with a little oil, sprinkle with the salt, and massage the kale for about 30 seconds. This will make the kale softer. And it's fun. Once the kale is "relaxed," add about ¼ cup of the dressing to the bowl and toss to coat the kale evenly. (Leftover dressing will keep in a covered container in the refrigerator for up to 5 days.)

Divide the dressed kale among four salad plates. Garnish with the tomatoes, radishes, and cheese, dividing them evenly, and then finish each salad with a crack of pepper. Enjoy with wine. Toga optional.

TASTY SALAD OR
MODERN ART

A LANCE FAVORITE (BUT WHO DOESN'T LOVE A WEDGE?)

# the "wine wednesday" wedge

A nice crisp wedge salad is one of the best ways to start a "wine adventure" with friends. That's because it's easy to make and even easier to enjoy with a glass of chilled white wine, like our iconic *James Gang Reserve* Chardonnay. Kick off your evening with this bold, flavorful salad (and the homemade ranch dressing!), which will set the stage for a heck of a great night. Why is this salad called The "Wine Wednesday" Wedge? Wine not?!

## WINE PAIRING

*James Gang Reserve* Chardonnay

*Ballistic* Zinfandel

**PREP TIME**
35 TO 45 MINUTES

**MAKES**
4 SERVINGS

GF

## RANCH DRESSING

½ cup sour cream

½ cup buttermilk

1 cup mayonnaise

¾ tsp garlic powder

¾ tsp onion powder

¾ tsp fresh lime juice

1 Tbsp sugar (optional)

1½ tsp chopped fresh flat-leaf parsley leaves, or ½ tsp dried parsley

1½ tsp chopped fresh tarragon leaves, or ½ tsp dried tarragon

Kosher salt and freshly ground black pepper

## SALAD

1 head iceberg lettuce

12 cherry tomatoes, halved

1 cup pitted Castelvetrano olives, quartered

1 cup diced English cucumber

½ cup crumbled blue cheese

½ cup chopped cooked bacon (from about 8 slices)

½ cup Pickled Red Onions (page 211)

½ cup loosely packed fresh dill fronds

### make the ranch dressing

In a large bowl, whisk together the sour cream, buttermilk, mayonnaise, garlic powder, onion powder, lime juice, and sugar (if using). Fold in the parsley and tarragon and season with salt and pepper. Cover and chill for at least 30 minutes to allow the flavors to blend. (You will have more dressing than you need for the wedges. The leftover dressing will keep in a covered container in the refrigerator for up to 5 days.)

### make the salad

Remove the outer layer of leaves from the lettuce head, then cut out the core with a small, sharp knife. Using a large, sharp knife, quarter the head through the stem end. Place the quarters, rounded side down, on four salad plates or on a single large platter.

Spoon ¼ cup of the dressing over the peak of each wedge and let it drip down both sides.

Divide the tomatoes, olives, cucumber, blue cheese, bacon, and pickled onions evenly among the wedges, arranging them atop and next to the lettuce. Finish with the dill, dividing it evenly. Serve immediately. People are hungry and they want their wedge!

**CHEF PRO TIP:** Wedge salads are an easy way to impress your friends, and it's one of Lance's indulgent favorites!

VEGGIE BACON?! YUP.

## DRESSING

½ cup diced peeled carrot

½ small yellow onion, diced

2 Tbsp minced peeled fresh ginger

¼ cup soy sauce or tamari

¼ cup rice vinegar

2 Tbsp Dijon mustard

¼ cup toasted sesame oil

¼ cup extra-virgin olive oil

## SHIITAKE "BACON"

3½ oz shiitake mushrooms, stemmed and cut into ¼-inch-wide slices

½ cup low-sodium soy sauce

1 Tbsp toasted sesame oil

## ONION CUPS

1 whole yellow onion

1 Tbsp grapeseed oil

## CARAMELIZED ONIONS

2 Tbsp unsalted butter

3 cups diced or julienned yellow onions

Kosher salt and freshly ground black pepper

## SALAD

2 medium heads Bibb lettuce

1 cup walnut pieces, toasted

1 cup sliced hearts of palm, in half-moons

1 cup diced roasted red bell peppers

½ cup peeled and diced Persian cucumber

2 Tbsp sliced fresh chives

2 Tbsp fresh cilantro leaves

12 fresh basil leaves

# shiitake "bacon" lettuce cups

This is a 100 percent vegan dish. That's right. You're going to learn how to make shiitake "bacon" that will impress your vegan friends and might even convert a few carnivores. Shiitake mushrooms are a great substitute for bacon because they're packed with meaty umami flavor. Add the salt from the soy sauce and the smoky nuttiness from the sesame oil and you've got a bacon-inspired topping that will complement most hearty salads. Raise a glass of *Radiance* Chardonnay and toast to your health with this totally plant-based dish.

## WINE PAIRING

*Radiance* **Chardonnay**

*James Gang Reserve* **Riesling**

---

**PREP TIME**
25 TO 35 MINUTES

---

**COOK TIME**
45 TO 50 MINUTES

---

**MAKES**
4 SERVINGS

---

**GF/VEG/VG**

### make the dressing

In a blender, combine all of the ingredients except the olive oil and blend on high speed for 30 seconds. With the blender running on low speed, slowly add the olive oil until the mixture emulsifies and is smooth and creamy. If the dressing is too thick, thin with a little water and blend on low speed. Set the dressing aside.

### make the shiitake "bacon"

Preheat the oven to 450°F.

In a small bowl, mix together the mushrooms, soy sauce, and sesame oil and let marinate for about 5 minutes. Drain well, then spread the mushrooms in a single layer on a sheet pan. Line a second sheet pan with paper towels.

Bake the mushrooms until crisp (but not burned), 8 to 10 minutes. Pay close attention, as they can burn really quickly. Transfer the shiitake pieces to the towel-lined sheet pan and let cool. The shiitake "bacon" will harden more as it cools.

---

**CHEF PRO TIP:** This shiitake "bacon" works well on all kinds of salad. It also goes beautifully with spinach and feta!

---

### make the onion cups

Leave the oven set at 450°F. Heat a small cast-iron frying pan on the stove top over medium heat. While the pan is heating, cut the onion in half lengthwise (from stem to root) and peel off the skin from each half.

Add the grapeseed oil to the hot pan, and when the oil begins to smoke lightly, add the onion halves, cut side down, and sear until golden brown, about 2 minutes. Transfer the pan to the oven and roast the onion halves until cooked through and softened, about 20 minutes.

Remove the pan from the oven. Gently remove the onion halves from the pan. The cut sides should be charred and very dark. Once the onion halves cool, separate them into onion "petal" cups (see photo). These cups will hold the extra dressing.

### make the caramelized onions

In a large cast-iron pan over medium heat, melt the butter. Add the diced onions, stir gently to coat with the butter, and cook, stirring often, until they are golden brown and delicious, about 20 minutes. Season with salt and pepper. Remove from the heat and let cool.

### make the salad

Trim away the core from the lettuce heads and separate and wash the leaves. You need three good leaves for each serving.

In a medium bowl, combine the caramelized onions, walnuts, hearts of palm, roasted peppers, cucumbers, and about half the dressing (about ¾ cup) and mix well with a spoon.

Lay three lettuce leaves on each salad plate. Using a large spoon, divide the onion mixture evenly among all the lettuce leaves. Top each lettuce cup with the shiitake "bacon," chives, cilantro, and basil, dividing them evenly. Place the onion cups next to the lettuce cups on each plate and serve the remaining dressing in the onion cups.

Silverware optional! For a little extra fun, don't tell your guests it's not real bacon until they're on their second glass of wine.

# soups

Above all else, wine is seasonal. There's a growing season and a harvest time. And each step along the way—from crush to blending to barrel aging—adds depth and character to the grapes for a taste that's wholly unique to every vintage. The best soups can be just as versatile as a great wine, especially when you pair them. Beat the summer heat with a chilled bottle of Sauvignon Blanc and a refreshing gazpacho made with vine-ripened tomatoes. Warm up on a chilly autumn evening with a glass of *James Gang Reserve Private Stash* and a heaping bowl of Beef & Barley Harvest Soup. Pair these soups with any of the entrées in this book to prime your palate and set the stage for an unforgettable evening, or enjoy each soup on its own. Yes, soup *can* be a meal. The recipes in this chapter are arranged from lighter to bolder soups and a hearty chili, so you can build the perfect meal to pair with your favorite red, white, or even rosé wine.

# california heirloom tomato gazpacho

**WINE PAIRING**

*Sundance*
Sauvignon Blanc

*RED* Blend

**PREP TIME**
20 TO 30 MINUTES (PLUS
2 HOURS TO CHILL)

**MAKES**
4 SERVINGS

**GF/VEG/VG**

Fresh, juicy heirloom tomatoes might just be the best thing about summer—right behind fireworks, warm nights, and a cool glass of crisp Sauvignon Blanc. The end of July to the beginning of September is the best time of year to find the tastiest heirloom tomatoes, so take the opportunity to wow your guests with an unforgettable—and unique—dish at your next backyard get-together. Because every heirloom tomato comes with its own distinctive flavor profile, don't be afraid to experiment a little. Vine-ripened beefsteak tomatoes are a favorite and work particularly well for this gazpacho. But as long as you get fresh *in-season* tomatoes, you can't go wrong.

1½ lb heirloom tomatoes, halved, seeded, and chopped

1 cup peeled, seeded, and chopped English cucumber

½ cup chopped red bell pepper

1 small jalapeño chile, seeded and minced (optional)

1 garlic clove, minced

¼ cup extra-virgin olive oil, plus 2 Tbsp for garnish

1 Tbsp fresh lime juice

2 tsp red wine vinegar

½ tsp toasted ground cumin (you can buy it or toast your own)

1 tsp kosher salt

¼ tsp freshly ground black pepper

¾ cup chopped red onion

Fresh basil or other fresh herbs you like for garnish

In a large bowl, combine the tomatoes, cucumber, bell pepper, chile (if using), garlic, oil, lime juice, vinegar, cumin, salt, and pepper. Then add ½ cup of the onion (save the rest for garnish) and mix everything together with a big spoon.

Transfer the mixture to a blender and blend on high speed, 30 to 60 seconds. You want a very smooth liquid. Transfer to an airtight container and chill for at least 2 hours but preferably overnight.

Before serving, taste the soup and season with salt and pepper if needed. To serve, divide the soup among four soup bowls and garnish each serving with the basil, the remaining ¼ cup onion, and a drizzle of oil for that extra-smooth finish.

**CHEF PRO TIP:** Never put whole fresh tomatoes in the fridge. It will ruin their texture and flavor.

HOW CLAIRE "CHILLS"

# chilled pea & mint soup

This is *the* quintessential spring dish. Fresh. Vibrant. Aromatic. Each spoonful of this chilled soup is a breath of freshness. Great for warmer days and light wine, pair it with a glass of *James Gang Reserve* Riesling and enjoy the notes of lemongrass, white peach, and dreams of sunny days. It's also just a really darn tasty soup.

3 Tbsp unsalted butter

1 cup chopped yellow onion

Kosher salt and freshly ground black pepper

Two 16 oz bags frozen green peas, or 6 cups shelled fresh green peas, blanched

¼ cup loosely packed fresh mint leaves, plus more for garnish

1 cup plain full-fat Greek yogurt

3 Tbsp extra-virgin olive oil

2 Tbsp chopped fresh chives

In a medium, heavy pot over low heat, melt the butter. Add onion and cook, stirring often, until softened but not browned, 6 to 8 minutes. Add 1 tsp salt and 2 cups water, stir to mix, and bring to a boil over high heat. Remove from the heat.

Add the peas and ¼ cup mint to the pot and then stir in the yogurt. Working in two batches, transfer the mixture to a stand blender and blend on high speed until smooth. Alternatively, purée the soup directly in the pot using an immersion blender. If the soup is too thick, thin it with water as needed. Season with salt and pepper and let cool to room temperature.

Transfer to an airtight container and chill for at least 2 hours but preferably overnight.

**CHEF PRO TIP:** You can chill this soup for up to 2 days before serving.

Before serving, taste the soup and season with salt and pepper as needed. To serve, divide the soup among four to six soup bowls and top each serving with a swirl of the oil, the mint and chives, and a grind or two of pepper. If you bought chives with the blossoms intact (or harvested them from your own herb garden), save some of the flowers for an extra-special garnish.

**PREP TIME**
10 TO 15 MINUTES (PLUS 2 HOURS TO CHILL)

**COOK TIME**
10 TO 12 MINUTES

**MAKES**
4 TO 6 SERVINGS

**GF/VEG**

# madras curry carrot soup

Does curry spice really go well with wine? Absolutely! The natural sweetness of carrots cuts through the complex curry spice for an enticing contrast of exotic flavors. Dare to pair this heavenly soup with our bright *Radiance* Chardonnay, or with our *James Gang Reserve* Riesling for an even sweeter finish to complement the lingering spices.

**WINE PAIRING**

*Radiance* Chardonnay

*James Gang Reserve* Riesling

2 Tbsp grapeseed oil or coconut oil

½ cup diced yellow onion

1 Tbsp Madras curry powder

1 tsp garam masala

1 Tbsp minced garlic

1 Tbsp minced peeled fresh ginger

2 cups diced peeled carrots

½ cup diced fennel (about 1 bulb)

½ cup diced celery

½ cup diced leek, white part only

1 cup small cauliflower florets

½ cup raw cashews

3 cups chicken stock or vegetable stock, homemade (page 206) or purchased

Kosher salt and freshly ground black pepper

Microgreens, such as sunflower sprouts or fennel fronds, for garnish (optional)

Extra-virgin olive oil for garnish

In a large, heavy pot over medium-high heat, warm the grapeseed oil until it begins to smoke lightly. Add the onion and cook, stirring often, until golden brown and delicious, about 5 minutes. Add the curry powder, garam masala, garlic, and ginger and cook, stirring, to toast the spices lightly, about 1 minute. Add the carrots, fennel, celery, leek, and cauliflower and cook, stirring occasionally, just until the vegetables begin to soften, about 2 minutes.

**CHEF PRO TIP:** Use the acronym GBD— aka golden brown and delicious—around your chef friends. They'll love it.

Add the cashews and stock to the pot, bring the mixture to a simmer, and simmer until all the vegetables soften, 10 to 15 minutes. They should be soft enough to smoosh with a spoon on a cutting board.

Remove from the heat and let cool for a couple of minutes. Fill a blender half full with the soup and blend on high speed until smooth. Repeat until all the soup is puréed.

Transfer the soup back to the pot and bring to a simmer over medium-low heat until hot, 3 to 5 minutes. To serve, season with salt and pepper and divide among four soup bowls. For a bit of extra flair, top each bowl with a few microgreens (if using) and an oh-so-stylish drizzle of olive oil.

**PREP TIME**
30 MINUTES

**COOK TIME**
25 TO 30 MINUTES

**MAKES**
4 SERVINGS

GF/VEG/VG

# james gang tuscan white bean soup

A simple, clean-tasting, healthy alternative to heavy stews, this delicious Italian-inspired soup pairs beautifully with our Italian-style wines. So, if you're craving a light meal to go with a great bottle of wine (hint hint, Tobin James), you've found it. You can even make this soup vegan by leaving out the Parmesan cheese. And remember, as Julia Child famously said, "I enjoy cooking with wine. Sometimes, I even put it in the food."

## WINE PAIRING

*James Gang Reserve* **Chardonnay**

*Primo* **Sangiovese**

*Pasorolo* **Nebbiolo**

2 Tbsp extra-virgin olive oil, plus more for garnish

1 cup finely diced yellow onion

½ cup finely diced peeled carrot

1 cup finely diced celery

4 garlic cloves, minced

¼ tsp red pepper flakes

1 cup **James Gang Reserve Chardonnay**

4 cups vegetable stock, homemade (page 206) or purchased

Two 15 oz cans cannellini or Great Northern beans, with their liquid

Four 6-inch fresh rosemary sprigs, leaves stripped and finely chopped and stems reserved

2 bay leaves

3- by 4-inch piece Parmesan cheese rind (optional)

Kosher salt and freshly ground black pepper

2 Tbsp thinly sliced fresh chives

In a large saucepan over medium-high heat, warm the oil. Add the onion, carrot, and celery and cook, stirring frequently, until softened but not browned, about 3 minutes. Add the garlic and red pepper flakes and cook, stirring constantly, until fragrant, about 1 minute. Add the wine, bring to a simmer, and cook uncovered until the wine has nearly evaporated, 3 to 5 minutes.

Add the stock, beans and their liquid, rosemary stems (save the leaves for garnish), bay leaves, and Parmesan rind (if using), raise the heat to high, and bring to a boil. Turn down the heat to low, cover, and simmer gently for 15 minutes to blend the flavors.

Remove and discard the bay leaves, rosemary stems, and Parmesan rind. Using an immersion blender, roughly purée part of the beans until you get a soup consistency you like. Alternatively, transfer 2 cups of the soup to a stand blender and blend until smooth (start on low speed and increase to high to prevent blender blowout), then return the purée to the soup and stir to combine.

Season the soup with salt and pepper. To serve, divide among four to six soup bowls and sprinkle with as much chopped rosemary as you like and the chives. Drizzle each serving with a little oil to make it look extra fancy. Cheers!

**PREP TIME**
15 TO 20 MINUTES

**COOK TIME**
25 TO 30 MINUTES

**MAKES**
4 TO 6 SERVINGS

**GF/VEG/VG**

# the guest house

**The ultimate winery escape available only to our wine club members. The original stagecoach stop on our property has been remodeled into three fabulous suites, each uniquely themed and designed by the owners.**

ALL THAT'S MISSING IS YOU

Sun Room

Bordello Room

Tobin James Suite

## SOUP

2 Tbsp grapeseed oil

2 cups diced yellow onions

1 cup chopped cauliflower

1 cup diced celery

2 Tbsp diced shallot

5 garlic cloves, minced

2 cups chopped stemmed fresh shiitake mushrooms

1 cup chopped fresh portobello mushrooms

1 cup walnut pieces

4 cups chicken or vegetable stock, homemade (page 206) or purchased

¼ cup dried porcini mushrooms (optional)

Kosher salt and freshly ground black pepper

## GARNISH

2 Tbsp grapeseed oil

1 cup diced stemmed fresh shiitake mushrooms (gills removed)

4 fresh trumpet mushrooms, sliced lengthwise

Kosher salt and freshly ground black pepper

½ cup walnut pieces, toasted and chopped

2 Tbsp chopped fresh flat-leaf parsley

Extra-virgin olive oil or truffle oil

# fat fungi mushroom soup

This meaty umami bomb is a spectacular soup to kick-start your next wine-friendly dinner. Made with three uniquely flavorful mushrooms and cauliflower for a creamy yet dairy-free texture, this soup has an elegant mouth-feel and a rich umami flavor that will stimulate your taste buds. Great for hard-core mushroom lovers and newbies alike, pair this earthy soup with a robust red like our legendary *Fat Boy* Zinfandel. *Fat Boy* and Fat Fungi soup are like best friends on a seesaw—perfectly balanced and nothing but fun. You can't enjoy one without the other.

**PREP TIME**
15 TO 20 MINUTES

**COOK TIME**
30 TO 40 MINUTES

**MAKES**
4 SERVINGS

**GF/VEG/VG**

### make the soup

In a medium heavy saucepan over medium heat, warm the grapeseed oil until it begins to smoke lightly. Add the onion and cook, stirring often, until golden brown, 5 to 8 minutes. Add the cauliflower, celery, shallot, garlic, shiitake and porto-bello mushrooms, and walnuts and cook, stirring constantly to prevent burning, until cooked through and softened, about 5 minutes.

Add the stock and porcini mushrooms, if using, and simmer over medium heat until all the vegetables start to soften, about 15 minutes. Remove from the heat and let cool for 10 minutes. While the soup cools, make the garnish.

### make the garnish

In a medium sauté pan over medium heat, warm the grape-seed oil. Add the shiitake and trumpet mushrooms and cook, stirring occasionally, until browned, 3 to 5 minutes. Remove from the heat and season with salt and pepper, then stir in the walnuts and parsley.

Working in batches, transfer the partially cooled soup to a blender and blend on high speed until smooth. Return the puréed soup to the pot, season with salt and pepper, and bring to a gentle boil over medium heat, about 1 minute. After that, the soup is ready to serve.

To serve, divide the hot soup among four soup bowls. Garnish each serving with one-fourth of the mushroom mixture and a drizzle of olive oil—or truffle oil if you're feeling fancy—and enjoy with a glass of *Fat Boy* **Zin**! You've earned it.

# provençal lentil soup

The secret to a great lentil soup is simple. You just need to use authentic French lentils (the small green ones). They hold their shape better than brown lentils, so there's no risk of a mushy soup. They also cook a little faster (thank goodness!). But the real reason we love French lentil soup is because of how beautifully it pairs with wine. The earthy taste and slight minerality of green lentils match well with our red **GSM** Blend or with a more subtle white, like our **James Gang Reserve** Chardonnay.

**WINE PAIRING**

*James Gang Reserve* Chardonnay

*GSM* Blend

**PREP TIME**
20 TO 25 MINUTES

**COOK TIME**
1 HOUR

**MAKES**
4 SERVINGS

**GF/VEG/VG**

1½ tsp grapeseed oil

1 cup diced yellow onion

½ cup diced celery, plus leaves for garnish

½ cup diced peeled carrot

½ red bell pepper, seeded and diced

4 garlic cloves, minced

1½ tsp herbes de Provence

4½ cups chicken stock or vegetable stock, homemade (page 206) or purchased

1 cup dried French green lentils, rinsed

1½ tsp tomato paste

½ cup diced fresh or canned tomatoes

Kosher salt and freshly ground black pepper

In a large saucepan over medium-high heat, warm the oil. Add the onion, celery, carrot, and bell pepper and cook, stirring often, until the vegetables begin to brown, about 15 minutes.

Add the garlic and herbes de Provence and cook, stirring, for 1 minute. Then add the stock, lentils, and tomato paste, stir well, and bring to a simmer. Turn down the heat to medium-low, cover, and simmer gently until the lentils are tender, about 35 minutes.

---

**CHEF PRO TIP:** French lentils are the secret to great lentil soup. Do your best to find authentic French green lentils, which are native to the Auvergne region, and half the work is already done!

Using an immersion blender, roughly purée part of the lentils until you get a soup consistency you like. Alternatively, transfer 2 cups of the soup to a stand blender and blend until smooth (start on low speed and increase to high to prevent blender blowout), then return the purée to the soup and stir to combine.

Add the diced tomatoes and simmer over low heat for 1 minute. Check to see if the soup nicely coats the back of a spoon. If it's too thick, thin it with more stock or with water. Season with salt and pepper.

To serve, divide the soup among four soup bowls and garnish each serving with celery leaves, then raise a glass of buttery *James Gang Reserve* **Chardonnay** or robust *GSM*.

WEDDING NOT REQUIRED

## MEATBALLS

8 oz ground chicken, preferably dark meat

8 oz fresh chicken sausage (not smoked), casings removed, or ground chicken (preferably dark meat)

⅓ cup panko bread crumbs

¼ cup grated Parmesan cheese

1 egg

½ tsp dried oregano

½ tsp dried basil

½ tsp dried parsley

¼ tsp garlic powder

Kosher salt and freshly ground black pepper

1 Tbsp extra-virgin olive oil

## SOUP

1 Tbsp extra-virgin olive oil

2 cups diced yellow onions

1 cup diced peeled carrots

1 cup diced celery

3 garlic cloves, minced

½ tsp dried thyme

8 cups chicken stock, homemade (page 206) or purchased

2 bay leaves

½ cup *acini di pepe* pasta

1 fresh rosemary sprig

3 cups chopped baby spinach

1 Tbsp fresh lemon juice

2 Tbsp chopped fresh flat-leaf parsley leaves

Kosher salt and freshly ground black pepper

4 tablespoons grated Parmesan cheese (optional)

# italian wine & wedding soup

Italian wedding soup is one of our all-time favorite soup recipes, especially in fall. The hearty combination of handmade meatballs, diced vegetables, and delicate pasta in a rich, flavorful broth that marries with our *Ballistic* Zin is about as good as it gets. Why is it called Italian wedding soup? While it's fun to imagine Italian newlyweds in Tuscany slurping spoonfuls of meatball soup on their big day, the "married" part simply refers to the original Italian name for the soup, *minestra maritata*, or "married soup."

## WINE PAIRING

*Ballistic* **Zinfandel**

*James Gang* **Reserve Primitivo**

**PREP TIME**
1 HOUR

**COOK TIME**
30 MINUTES

**MAKES**
4 SERVINGS

### make the meatballs

In a large bowl, combine the ground chicken, chicken sausage, bread crumbs, cheese, egg, oregano, basil, parsley, and garlic powder and season with salt and pepper. Using a wooden spoon (or really clean hands if you like to get into it), stir until all the ingredients are well mixed.

Using your palms, roll the mixture into ¾- to 1-inch balls. You should have 25 to 30 meatballs. If you're running out of meat, just make your meatballs smaller. Remember, larger meatballs might look great, but they'll be harder to cook all the way through and might not fit into a soup bowl as well.

**CHEF PRO TIP:** Less is more when it comes to Italian wedding soup. Smaller meatballs and al dente pasta are the way to go! Speaking of pasta, if you cannot find *acini di pepe*—literally "seeds of pepper" aka peppercorns— another small pasta shape can be substituted, such as *tubettini* (little tubes) and *seme di melone* (melon seeds).

Line a large plate with paper towels and set it near the stove. In a Dutch oven or large stockpot (at least 4 qt) over medium heat, warm the oil. Working in small batches, add the meatballs and cook, turning as needed, until browned on all sides, 2 to 3 minutes. As each batch is ready, using a slotted spoon, transfer the meatballs to the towel-lined plate. Set the browned meatballs aside.

### make the soup

In the same pot over medium heat, warm the oil. Add the onions, carrots, celery, and garlic and cook, stirring occasionally, until tender, 3 to 4 minutes. Stir in the thyme and cook, stirring once or twice, until fragrant, about 1 minute.

Whisk in the stock and bay leaves, raise the heat to high, and bring everything to a boil. Stir in the pasta, rosemary, and meatballs, turn down the heat to low, and simmer until the pasta is al dente and the meatballs are cooked through, 9 to 12 minutes.

Stir in the spinach, lemon juice, and parsley and simmer until the spinach has wilted, about 30 seconds. Season with salt and pepper.

To serve, divide the soup among four soup bowls and garnish each serving with 1 tablespoon of the cheese—or skip the cheese if you like. Serve immediately. Italian wedding soup tastes best when it is freshly made. Dive in and make a mess— hopefully, you're not wearing your wedding dress!

# *primo* minestrone

Chunky, earthy, homey—there's a reason you have fond memories of minestrone soup. Because it's what home cooking is supposed to taste like. Our minestrone is all about blending simple ingredients and rich, hearty flavors to become more than the sum of their parts. No matter how you pronounce it, minestrone always goes better with a glass of wine.

⅓ cup elbow pasta

2 Tbsp extra-virgin olive oil, plus more for serving

2 cups diced yellow onions

1 cup diced celery

1 cup diced peeled carrots

4 garlic cloves, minced

1 tsp dried oregano

1 tsp dried basil

One 28-oz can diced tomatoes, with juices

One 14-oz can crushed tomatoes , with juices

4 cups chicken stock or vegetable stock, homemade (page 206) or purchased

8 oz fresh green beans, trimmed and halved crosswise (1½ cups)

One 14-oz can red kidney beans, drained

Kosher salt and freshly ground black pepper

⅓ cup grated pecorino romano cheese

2 Tbsp chopped fresh basil leaves

Step 1: Pour yourself a glass of *Primo* **Sangiovese**.

Step 2: Select "Italian Cooking Music" on Spotify.

Step 3: Belt out the "lyrics" to that one song. You know the one. *"Funiculi, Funicula!"*

Step 4: Make the soup.

Fill a medium saucepan with water and bring to a boil over high heat. Add the pasta and cook according to the package directions. Drain and set aside until needed.

In a large stockpot over medium heat, warm the oil. Add the onions, celery, and carrots and cook, stirring occasionally, until the vegetables start to brown lightly, 5 to 8 minutes. Add the garlic, oregano, and dried basil and cook, stirring, for 2 more minutes.

Add the diced and crushed tomatoes, stock, green beans, and kidney beans to the pot, turn down the heat to low, and simmer, uncovered, stirring occasionally to make sure nothing sticks to the bottom, until the green beans are tender and the flavors are blended, about 20 minutes. Pour yourself a glass of *Primo* **Sangiovese** to keep you company while everything simmers.

When you're ready to serve, add a small amount of the cooked pasta. You can always add more later. The pasta will soak up the soup fairly quickly, so wait until the last minute to add more pasta to the pot. Season the soup with salt and pepper.

To serve, divide the soup among four to six soup bowls and garnish with the cheese and fresh basil, dividing them evenly. Finish each bowl with a silky drizzle of oil and serve. *Buon appetito!*

---

**CHEF PRO TIP:** Cook the minestrone soup a day ahead of time to give the ingredients time to "get to know each other in the pot."

---

**PREP TIME**
20 TO 30 MINUTES

**COOK TIME**
35 TO 40 MINUTES

**MAKES**
4 TO 6 SERVINGS

**VEG**

# the grotto

Step into our grotto and immerse yourself in an artistic paradise. Crafted by local artisans, our warm and inviting space and authentic Italian pizza oven are beloved features at all of our parties.

PERFECT PICNIC SPOT!

# winemaker's chicken tortilla soup

This is quite possibly the most "Californian" soup in this cookbook (it's even got avocados!), which is probably why it pairs so well with our quintessentially Californian *James Gang Reserve* Zin. And if you're out of Tobin James, don't worry. Just grab every winemaker's favorite beverage during harvest—an ice-cold beer!

**WINE PAIRING**

*James Gang Reserve* Zinfandel

(or grab a beer!)

**PREP TIME**
10 TO 15 MINUTES

**COOK TIME**
30 TO 40 MINUTES

**MAKES**
4 TO 6 SERVINGS

GF

## SOUP

6 Tbsp grapeseed oil

Eight 6-inch corn tortillas, halved and cut into ¼-inch-wide strips

1 yellow onion, chopped

4 large garlic cloves, smashed

1 Tbsp smoked paprika

2 Tbsp ground cumin

1 tsp ground coriander

1 tsp chili powder

¼ tsp cayenne pepper

6 cups chicken or vegetable stock, homemade (page 206) or purchased

One 28-oz can crushed tomatoes, with juices

2 bay leaves

2½ tsp kosher salt

¼ cup loosely packed fresh cilantro leaves (optional)

1¾ lb boneless, skinless chicken breasts, cut into ¾-inch pieces

## GARNISH

2 Tbsp crumbled Cotija cheese

1 avocado, halved, pitted, peeled, and diced

2 Tbsp toasted pepitas (pumpkin seeds)

Chopped fresh cilantro leaves (optional)

Lime wedges

### fry the tortilla strips

Line a large plate with paper towels. In a large, heavy pot over medium-high heat, warm the oil until it begins to smoke lightly. Add half of the tortilla strips and cook, stirring, until pale golden and crunchy, about 1 minute. Using a slotted spoon, transfer to the towel-lined plate. Repeat with the remaining tortilla strips.

### make the soup

Scoop out all but 2 Tbsp of the oil from the pot and turn down the heat to medium-low. Add the onion, garlic, paprika, cumin, coriander, chili powder, and cayenne and cook, stirring occasionally, until aromatic, about 5 minutes. Add the stock, tomatoes, bay leaves, salt, cilantro leaves (if using), and about one-third of the tortilla strips (you'll use the rest for garnish). Bring to a simmer and cook, uncovered, for 30 minutes to blend the flavors.

Remove from the heat, remove and discard the bay leaves, and let cool for a few minutes. Working in batches, add the soup to a blender and blend on high speed until smooth. Return the puréed soup to the pot, place over low heat, and bring to a simmer. Add the chicken and simmer until cooked through, 1 to 3 minutes. Remove from the heat.

**CHEF PRO TIP:** Blending in some of the tortilla strips gives the soup a creamier texture. You can also use smoked paprika for a little added warmth.

### serve the soup

Divide among four to six soup bowls and garnish each bowl with the remaining tortilla strips, the cheese, avocado, and pepitas, dividing them evenly, then finish with a sprinkle of cilantro (if using). Serve with the lime wedges and enjoy with a nice glass of *James Gang Reserve* Zinfandel or crack open that beer!

# *notorious* cuban black bean soup

One of the most "notorious" dishes in this book, our Cuban-inspired black bean soup is creamy, velvety, and packed with rich, earthy smoothness that demands your full attention. When cooked slowly so all the flavors meld, it becomes a subtle, sophisticated dish thanks to a little TLC. And it never hurts to add a dash of *Notorious* Cab to the recipe (and your glass!) to give your soup an extra kick!

## WINE PAIRING

*Notorious*
Cabernet
Sauvignon

**PREP TIME**
10 TO 15 MINUTES (PLUS OVERNIGHT SOAK)

**COOK TIME**
4 TO 5 HOURS

**MAKES**
4 TO 6 SERVINGS

GF

**SOUP**

1 lb dried black beans

¼ cup *Notorious* Cabernet Sauvignon

1 yellow onion, finely chopped

1 green bell pepper, seeded and finely chopped

3 garlic cloves, minced

1 ham bone or smoked ham hock

½ cup extra-virgin olive oil

2 tsp kosher salt

Freshly ground black pepper

¼ cup distilled white or apple cider vinegar

Cooked white rice for serving (optional)

**GARNISH (OPTIONAL)**

Sour cream

Chopped red onion

Chopped green onions, white and green parts

Chopped red bell pepper

Espelette pepper or smoked paprika

### soak the beans

The night before, rinse the beans in a colander under running cold water. Pick out any tiny rocks and broken or shriveled beans.

In a large, heavy pot, combine the rinsed beans with cold water to cover by at least 1 inch. Cover with a lid and soak overnight at room temperature. Sample a glass of *Notorious Cab* to make sure it still tastes fantastic. Soaking beans is hard work.

### make the soup

The next day, drain the beans, return them to the pot, and add water to cover by 1 inch. Add the wine, onion, bell pepper, garlic, ham bone, oil, salt, and a generous quantity of black pepper. Stir to combine, then bring to a boil over high heat. Skim off any white foam that forms on the surface, then turn down the heat to low, cover, and simmer until the beans are very soft and the liquid is creamy rather than watery. This usually takes 4 to 5 hours, but you should check on the soup after about 2 hours to make sure the beans are still covered with water. If the beans seem dry or too much water has boiled off, add another cup of water. The goal is to continue cooking the soup until some of the beans break down and create a smooth, thick soup base. The soup should have a velvety, thick consistency. You'll know you're on the right track if the soup coats the back of a spoon.

When the soup is nearly finished, uncover, stir in the vinegar, and simmer, uncovered, for 15 minutes. Pull the ham bone out of the pot. The meat that hasn't already fallen off of it should be easy to pick off. Coarsely chop the meat and return it to the pot.

Working in batches, transfer the soup to a blender and blend on high speed until smooth. Return the puréed soup to the pot, season with salt and pepper, and bring to a gentle boil over medium heat, about 1 minute. After that, the soup is ready to serve.

### serve the soup

For a little added texture (or not, it's up to you), add a good-size scoop of rice to each soup bowl, then ladle the soup over the rice. If using, garnish each serving with sour cream, red onion, green onions, bell pepper, and a pinch of Espelette pepper. Serve at once.

Raise what's left of your glass—hopefully, you've been enjoying some *Notorious* Cab during the cooking process!—and get ready for a rich, luxurious meal that's almost as smooth as the wine you'll be sipping.

# beef & barley harvest soup

Do you like wine? Do you like beef? If your answer to both questions is yes, you're going to *love* this soup. The mixture of chuck roast, ancient grain barley, and chanterelle mushrooms yields naturally nutty, earthy flavors that are made for one another. And pairing this soup with wine is a snap. This hearty slow-cooked classic matches well with just about any red. In fact, this soup is so filling and flavorful, you can (and should) make a meal of it.

## WINE PAIRING

*Chateau Le Cacheflo*

*Pasorolo* Nebbiolo

*Private Stash*

**PREP TIME**
30 TO 40 MINUTES

**COOK TIME**
1½ TO 2 HOURS

**MAKES**
4 TO 6 SERVINGS

3 Tbsp grapeseed oil

2 lb chuck roast, trimmed of excess fat and cut into ¾-inch cubes

Kosher salt and freshly ground black pepper

2 cups chopped yellow onions

1½ cups chopped, peeled carrots

1½ cups chanterelle, shiitake (stemmed), or portobello mushrooms

1 cup chopped celery

3 Tbsp tomato paste

4 garlic cloves, minced

2 cups chicken stock, homemade (page 206) or purchased

2 cups beef stock, homemade (page 207) or purchased

1 Tbsp low-sodium soy sauce

2 tsp Worcestershire sauce

2 tsp minced fresh rosemary, or ½ tsp dried rosemary

2 tsp minced fresh thyme, or ½ tsp dried thyme

1 cup pearled barley

3 Tbsp minced fresh flat-leaf parsley

In a large, heavy pot over medium-high heat, warm 1 Tbsp of the oil. While the oil heats, dab the beef cubes dry with a paper towel and season with salt and pepper. When the oil is hot, add half of the beef cubes, making sure not to crowd them in the pot. Sear until golden brown on the bottom, about 3 minutes. Once the bottom is browned, flip each piece and cook for 1 more minute.

**CHEF PRO TIP:** If you crowd the pan when you are searing beef, the meat will steam, which will turn it gray. Gray = bad. Brown = good.

Transfer the beef and its juices to a large plate. Add 1 Tbsp of the oil to the pot, and when the oil is hot, sear the remaining beef the same way and add it and its juices to the plate.

With the pot still over medium-high heat, add the remaining 1 Tbsp oil. Add the onions, carrots, mushrooms, and celery and cook, stirring occasionally, until lightly browned, about 3 minutes. Then add the tomato paste and garlic and cook, stirring, for 1 more minute.

Add the chicken and beef stock, soy sauce, Worcestershire sauce, rosemary, and thyme and then return the beef to the pot along with the juices on the plate. That's flavor, baby. Adjust the heat to medium, bring the mixture to a simmer, then reduce the heat to low, cover, and simmer until the beef is fairly tender. This usually takes 45 minutes to 1 hour. Keep an eye on the pot to make sure it doesn't boil.

Finally, add the barley, cover, and simmer until the barley is cooked thoroughly—soft yet chewy—20 to 40 minutes. Remove from the heat, season with salt and pepper, and stir in the parsley.

Divide among four to six soup bowls and serve with a glass of *Chateau Le Cacheflo*.

COOK-OFF CHAMP

# *ballistic* flank steak chili

This is *not* your average chili. Made with grilled flank steak, fire-roasted tomatoes, and our famous *Ballistic Zinfandel*, this chili is robust enough to serve as a main course—if you can find it in your heart to share with anyone else! The recipe comes from one of our famous Zinfest events, now called our James Gang Festival. The next day, we had a bunch of leftover flank steaks and wondered, what do you do with leftover flank steak? Answer: You put it in chili, of course! Although you grill the steak for the chili here, this recipe also works *incredibly well* with leftovers if you ever grill up too much steak. No matter how you make it, this balanced, meaty, flavor-packed chili is great for a hearty lunch in the backyard or a raucous dinner over a glass of Zin with friends. Open up a bottle, fire up the grill, and enjoy!

**WINE PAIRING**

*Ballistic* Zinfandel

(or any Tobin James Cellars Zinfandel!)

**PREP TIME**
15 TO 30 MINUTES

**COOK TIME**
45 TO 60 MINUTES

**MAKES**
4 TO 6 SERVINGS

**GF**

**STEAK**

1½ lb flank steak

Montreal steak seasoning or kosher salt and freshly ground black pepper

**CHILI**

2 Tbsp grapeseed oil

1 cup chopped yellow onion

1 cup chopped celery

2 garlic cloves, chopped

1 cup *Ballistic* Zinfandel

1 cup beef stock, homemade (page 207) or purchased

One 8 oz can tomato sauce

One 8 oz can diced fire-roasted tomatoes, with juices

1 Tbsp honey

2 Tbsp chili powder

1 tsp ground cumin

1 tsp kosher salt

¼ tsp cayenne pepper

One 15 oz can kidney beans, drained and rinsed

**GARNISH**

1 cup shredded or chunked Cheddar cheese

Chopped red onion

### grill the steak

Fire up the grill for direct grilling over high heat. Gas, wood, or charcoal all work great. Pull the flank out of the refrigerator 10 minutes before cooking. Generously season both sides with the Montreal seasoning.

Lightly brush the cooking grate with grapeseed oil to prevent the meat from sticking. Or dip a kitchen towel in grapeseed oil and rub the oil on the grate.

Cook the steak, turning once, for 6 to 8 minutes on each side for medium pink. Transfer to a plate and let rest. Save any juices from the steak. You'll use them in the chili!

### make the chili

In a large pot over medium heat, warm the oil until it begins to smoke lightly. Add the onion, celery, and garlic and cook, stirring occasionally, until browned, about 5 minutes. Add the wine and simmer, uncovered, until the liquid is almost gone, 5 to 10 minutes.

**CHEF PRO TIP:** When you add the wine, it might flame up a bit. Don't panic! That's the alcohol. It will burn off naturally.

While the wine is reducing, cut the steak into small cubes. Once it has reduced, add the stock, tomato sauce, tomatoes, honey, chili powder, cumin, salt, cayenne, and steak with juices to the pot and stir everything together well (don't be afraid to use a little elbow grease!). Bring to a simmer, then cover, turn down the heat to low, and simmer, stirring occasionally, for 30 minutes to blend the flavors. If the chili becomes too dry (aka too thick), add ½ cup water. Add the beans and continue to simmer over low heat for 10 minutes to heat the beans thoroughly.

To serve, divide among four to six soup bowls and garnish each bowl with the cheese and chopped onion. Serve at once and make room in your trophy case for this award-winning chili—a three-time champion of the Tobin James Cellars Chili Cook-Off!

entrées

The entrées in this section run the gamut from classic favorites to over-the-top feasts for your senses. But no matter which dishes you crave—or which Tobin James wines you love to drink—as long as you surround yourself with friends and family, you'll have everything you need for a memorable night. So grab a few friends and a great bottle of wine and get ready for some outstanding food and a few unforgettable nights!

YOU HAD ME AT QUINOA

# quinoa & hearts of palm cakes

We love this delicious vegan version of crab cakes. It is perfect for brunch or a light vegetarian meal because of how well the quinoa and hearts of palm pair with rosé and white wines. This can be your go-to, guilt-free, "healthy" daytime drinking dish. Rosé all day!

## WINE PAIRING

*Radiance* Chardonnay

*James Gang Reserve* Chardonnay

*Paradise* Rosé

**PREP TIME**
30 TO 45 MINUTES

**COOK TIME**
15 TO 20 MINUTES

**MAKES**
4 SERVINGS AS A MAIN DISH, OR 8 SERVINGS AS AN APPETIZER

GF/VEG/VG

## CASHEW MUSTARD SAUCE

½ cup raw cashews

1 Tbsp tahini

2 Tbsp whole-grain mustard

1 Tbsp lemon juice

½ cup extra-virgin olive oil

Kosher salt and freshly ground black pepper

## CAKES

About 4 Tbsp grapeseed oil

¼ cup diced yellow onion

¼ cup diced celery

¼ cup soy-free vegan mayonnaise

1 Tbsp yellow mustard

1 Tbsp Old Bay Seasoning

1 tsp garlic powder

One 15-oz can chickpeas, drained and rinsed

One 14-oz can hearts of palm, drained and sliced

1 cup cooked quinoa

¼ cup chopped fresh flat-leaf parsley

¼ cup sliced green onions, green and white parts

Kosher salt and freshly ground black pepper

### begin the sauce

In a small bowl, combine the cashews and ½ cup water and let soak for 30 minutes while you make the cakes.

### make the cakes

In a small frying pan over medium-high heat, warm 2 Tbsp of the grapeseed oil until the oil begins to smoke lightly. Add the onion and celery and cook, stirring occasionally, until golden brown, 2 to 3 minutes. Remove from the heat and let cool.

In a food processor, combine the mayonnaise, mustard, Old Bay, and garlic powder and pulse two or three times to mix. Add the chickpeas and hearts of palm and process for 30 seconds to chop and mix everything together.

Next, add the quinoa, parsley, and green onions and pulse five or six times to mix everything together. Do not purée it. It should have some texture. Transfer the mixture to a medium bowl and season with salt and pepper. Fold in the reserved onion and celery. Cover and refrigerate while you finish making the sauce. Rinse out the processor bowl.

### finish the sauce

In the food processor, combine the soaked cashews with their water, tahini, mustard, lemon juice, and olive oil and process for 1 minute. The sauce should be thick and creamy. Season with salt and pepper, then cover and refrigerate until serving.

### cook the cakes

Using a 3-inch round ring mold (or cookie cutter), shape the cakes. Each one will weigh 4 to 5 oz and be about 1½ inches thick. If you don't have a ring mold, shape them by hand like a burger patty. Be sure to pack the cakes tightly so they don't fall apart when you cook them. You should have eight cakes.

Line a sheet pan with paper towels and set it near the stove. In a large, nonstick frying pan over medium-high heat, warm about 1 Tbsp of the grapeseed oil until it begins to smoke lightly. Use enough oil to coat the bottom of the pan. Working in batches to avoid crowding, add the cakes to the hot oil and sear, turning once, until golden brown on both sides, about 1 minute on each side. Transfer the cakes to the towel-lined sheet pan. Repeat with the remaining cakes, adding more oil to the pan as needed.

**CHEF PRO TIP:** Don't try to cook more than four cakes at one time. Give 'em room! You can keep the cooked cakes warm in the oven on the lowest setting until all the cakes are done.

To serve, divide the cakes among individual plates and top with the chilled sauce. If you're feeling fancy, serve with roasted seasonal vegetables, lemon wedges, and an herb salad. Decadent and delish!

# brown butter pasta with ricotta salata

*Slam dunk!* Brown butter pasta might seem simple, but that's why it's so great. If you make this dish with exceptional ingredients like high-quality spaghetti, organic grass-fed butter, and top-notch crumbly ricotta salata, you don't need to dress it up in a heavy sauce. Rich caramel, nutty, and briny, with flavor that lasts. Pair this with your favorite Italian-style red for a dinner that's miles from the butter noodles you remember as a kid.

1 lb spaghetti

Kosher salt and freshly ground black pepper

2 Tbsp extra-virgin olive oil

1 cup unsalted butter

About 2 cups grated ricotta salata, mizithra, or Cotija cheese

2 cups loosely packed fresh basil leaves

In a large pot over high heat, bring 5 qt water to a rolling boil. Add 2 Tbsp salt and then add the spaghetti and stir to keep the noodles from sticking together. Cook until al dente, 8 to 12 minutes.

**CHEF PRO TIP #1:** The Italian term *al dente* literally means "to the tooth." What that means in the kitchen is to cook the pasta until it's still a little firm when you bite into it. Not crunchy, not soft—just right.

When the pasta is done to your liking, drain, transfer to a large bowl, and toss with the oil, coating the noodles evenly. Do *not* rinse the pasta under cold running water.

In a large, heavy frying pan over medium heat, melt the butter. The butter will slowly start to bubble and separate as it melts. Pay close attention as the butter melts. You have to stir it occasionally to prevent the milk solids in the butter from sticking to the pan and burning.

**CHEF PRO TIP #2:** Butter is basically just oil, milk solids, and water, so when you melt butter in a pan, you're toasting the milk solids in the butter oil, which gives the end result a rich, toasted, nutty, caramelly flavor.

After 2 to 3 minutes, the milk solids will start to brown and give off a pleasant nutty smell. Once you hit this point, add the pasta to the pan and toss it in all that delicious brown butter goodness, coating the noodles evenly as they warm. Once the noodles are warm, season with salt and plenty of pepper and toss again.

Divide the pasta among four to six warmed individual plates, then garnish with as much of the cheese as you like and top with the basil for a simple, delicious Italian-style classic. Don't forget your favorite vino. Now that's Primo!

OH MY...

entrées ✳ 109

# fresh pasta

**You'll need a pasta machine with a roller attachment to make these homemade pasta sheets.**

2 cups "00" or all-purpose flour

¼ tsp kosher salt

3 whole eggs

3 egg yolks, beaten

Semolina or all-purpose flour, for dusting

In a medium bowl, stir together the "00" flour and salt. Then dump the flour mixture onto a smooth, flat surface. A kitchen countertop is best, but a large, wooden cutting board also works.

Make a tall, conical mound of flour (photo 1). Then make a well in the middle of the cone (photos 2 and 3) with your fingers. Next, add the whole eggs (photo 4) to the well. Finally, add the egg yolks to the well. Beat the whole eggs and yolks together with a fork to start to incorporate the flour. The eggs will "grab" the flour as you stir. Try not to break the walls of your flour crater (photos 5 through 8).

When about half of the flour has been mixed with the eggs (photo 9), start to mix in more of the flour with your fingers until all the flour turns into a chunky mess (photos 10 through 12). It's a good thing. You want all the flour to stick together (photo 13). If there is any dry flour that is *not* sticking to the mass, add a little water. This will suck up any remaining dry flour.

Now it's time to knead the dough. Using the palm of your hand, knead the dough by pushing the mound away from you and then pulling it back toward you (photos 14 and 15). Rotate the dough a quarter turn and repeat the pushing and pulling motion. Continue kneading in this way until the dough is smooth, elastic, and a uniform color, 4 to 5 minutes. You'll end up with a firm, smooth ball of dough (photo 16).

Next, wrap the dough in plastic wrap and let it rest at room temperature for at least 30 minutes or up to 2 hours. Line a sheet pan with parchment paper and lightly dust the parchment with semolina flour. Set the pan aside. Set up your pasta machine.

After the dough rests, unwrap it (photo 17). Cut off one-fourth of the dough (photo 18). Rewrap the remaining dough and set aside (photo 19). Use the palm of your hand to flatten the dough into an oval about the same width (6 to 8 inches) as your pasta machine (photo 20).

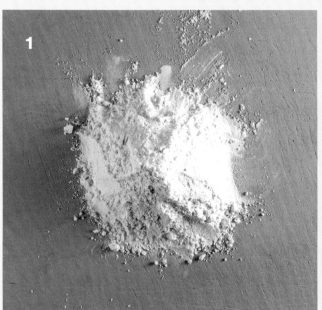

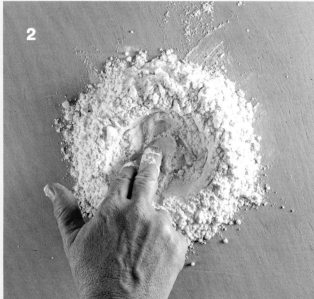

LIKE A VOLCANO!

Lightly flour a cutting board or countertop. Set the rollers to the widest setting and run the dough through the rollers (photo 21). Lay the dough out on the floured surface. Neatly fold each end of the dough rectangle inward into thirds—like folding a business letter—so the folded dough is the same width as the pasta machine (photo 22). Feed the pasta through the rollers *again* at the widest setting. Think of these first passes through the rollers as extended kneading.

Continue to fold the dough into thirds and roll it through the machine at the widest setting until it is smooth and evenly textured. Always make sure the folded dough is the full width of the machine.

At this point, you can stop folding the dough into thirds and begin to roll out the dough more thinly (photo 23). Roll it once through each of the next two or three narrower roller settings, dusting the pasta sheet with semolina flour as needed to prevent sticking, until the dough is about ¼ inch thick.

Now begin rolling the dough twice through each narrower setting. As you roll, lightly dust both sides of the pasta sheet with semolina flour to prevent it from sticking to itself.

CHEF PRO TIP: Roll out pasta until you can just see the outline of your hand when you hold it under a sheet, about ¹⁄₁₆ inch thick for noodles or ¹⁄₃₂ inch thick for filled pasta. (On most machines, you won't make it to the narrowest setting.)

Cut the finished pasta sheet into 12- to 14-inch-long pieces (photo 24). Dust them lightly with semolina flour, stack them on the parchment-lined sheet pan, and cover with a lightly dampened, clean kitchen towel. Repeat with the remaining three dough portions. You should end up with six to eight 12- to 14-inch-long sheets.

Once all the dough is rolled out, it's time to cut the sheets into noodles or to make stuffed pasta. If you are not ready to use them right away, flour the sheets well then wrap the pan tightly with plastic wrap or transfer the pasta sheets to an airtight container. Store in the refrigerator for up to 24 hours.

**PREP TIME**
45 TO 60 MINUTES

**MAKES**
SIX TO EIGHT 12- TO
14-INCH SHEETS

**VEG**

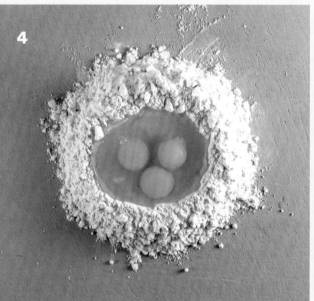
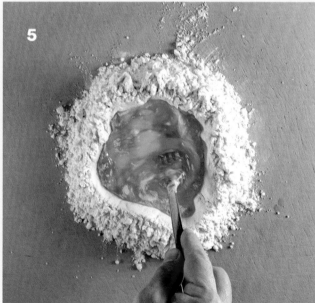

KNEADING TIME!

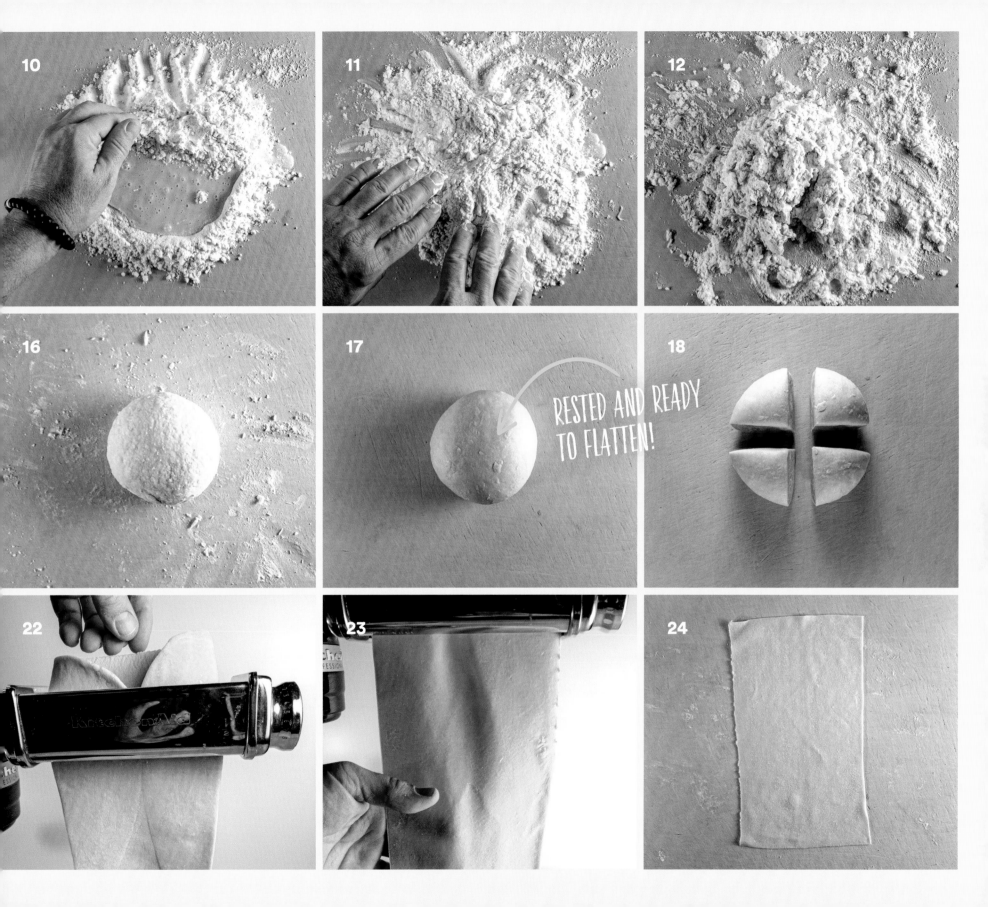

RESTED AND READY TO FLATTEN!

# bella bella black pepper fettuccine

You've had fettuccine Alfredo before. But not like this. A peppery riff on a timeless Italian classic, this velvety dish sets the stage for any Italian feast—especially if you have a few bottles of Tobin James handy.

Four 12- to 14-inch fresh pasta sheets (page 110) or 1 lb fresh fettuccine

Semolina or all-purpose flour, for dusting

1 cup *James Gang Reserve Chardonnay*

½ cup minced yellow onion, or 1 tsp onion powder

½ tsp freshly ground black pepper

1½ cups heavy cream

1 cup grated pecorino romano cheese, plus more for garnish

Kosher salt

Extra-virgin olive oil for drizzling

1 cup loosely packed fresh basil leaves

## cut the fettuccine

If your pasta machine has an attachment for cutting fettuccine, run the pasta sheets through the cutter and then dust the noodles with semolina. If your pasta machine does not have a cutter for fettuccine, starting from a narrow end, roll up each pasta sheet into a cylinder, then cut crosswise into strips ½ inch wide. Lift to unroll the noodles, then dust them with semolina. Place the noodles on a sheet pan and refrigerate until ready to use.

## make the sauce

Before starting the sauce, bring a large pot filled with 5 qt water to a rolling boil over high heat for cooking the pasta. In a medium saucepan over medium heat, combine the wine and onion, bring to a simmer, and simmer until the wine is almost entirely evaporated, 8 to 10 minutes. Add the pepper and stir to mix.

Add the cream, turn down the heat to low, and simmer until gently bubbling, 7 to 8 minutes. Watch constantly to make sure the cream sauce doesn't boil over. Turn off the heat and slowly whisk in the cheese until melted and fully incorporated. Cover and keep warm.

## cook the pasta

When the water in the large pot is at a rolling boil, add 1 Tbsp salt. Then add the noodles and stir gently to keep the noodles from sticking together. Cook the pasta for 2 to 3 minutes; it should be tender and cooked through, but not soft.

**CHEF PRO TIP #1:** Be careful not to crowd the pot. If you put too much pasta into the pot at once, it cools off the water too quickly. The best pasta has room to move in the convection of the water with a nice and steady temperature.

Drain the noodles. Drizzle with a little oil, top with a few grinds of pepper, and toss to coat.

**CHEF PRO TIP #2:** Tossing the noodles with just olive oil and pepper and serving them on top of the sauce allows diners to enjoy a few bites of the freshly made pasta without any sauce.

To serve, divide the warm sauce among four warmed individual plates or pour onto a serving platter and top with the noodles. Garnish with some cheese and the basil for a magnifico Italian-style feast.

## MUSHROOM FILLING

3 Tbsp grapeseed oil

10 oz shiitake mushrooms, stemmed and roughly chopped into ½-inch pieces (about 3 cups)

10 oz maitake mushrooms, roughly chopped into ½-inch pieces (about 3 cups)

½ cup diced yellow onion

6 garlic cloves, minced

½ cup Madeira wine

Kosher salt and freshly ground black pepper

1 cup whole-milk ricotta cheese

½ cup grated Parmesan cheese

1 egg

## SAUCE

1½ cups Madeira wine

2 cups Besciamella with Parmesan Cheese Sauce (page 210)

## RAVIOLI

All-purpose flour for dusting

Four 6- by 12-inch fresh pasta sheets (page 110)

1 egg

Kosher salt

Extra-virgin olive oil, for drizzling

1 cup loosely packed fresh basil leaves

# "the colossus" wild mushroom ravioli

This dish is literally just one big ravioli. Why? Because making ravioli by hand takes forever. So skip the hard part and get to the good stuff with one huge ravioli, leaving you with more time to eat and enjoy a glass of wine with friends. The earthy mushroom stuffing and creamy Parmesan sauce pair beautifully with our bold Italian reds, like the *Pasorolo* Nebbiolo. If you don't want to juggle making all the components the same day, you can make the fresh pasta and Besciamella with Parmesan sauce a day in advance.

**WINE PAIRING**

*Silver Reserve* Zinfandel

*Pasorolo* Nebbiolo

**PREP TIME**
45 TO 60 MINUTES, (PLUS 1 HOUR IF MAKING FRESH PASTA, AND 25 MINUTES TO MAKE THE BESCIAMELLA WITH PARMESAN CHEESE SAUCE)

**COOK TIME**
8 TO 12 MINUTES

**MAKES**
4 SERVINGS

**VEG**

### make the mushroom filling

In a sauté pan over high heat, warm the grapeseed oil until it begins to smoke lightly, about 1 minute. Add the mushrooms and sauté until golden brown, about 2 minutes. Remove one-third of the mushrooms from the pan and set them aside.

Turn down the heat to medium, add the onion and garlic, and cook, stirring often, until the onion is translucent and soft, about 2 minutes. Add the wine and simmer until the wine is almost entirely evaporated. Remove from the heat. Season with salt and pepper and then transfer to a heatproof container and let cool for a minute or two. Refrigerate for 10 minutes.

Transfer the chilled mushroom mixture to a food processor or blender. Add the ricotta, Parmesan, and egg and pulse eight to ten times to incorporate all the ingredients. You want a little texture to remain. Refrigerate until needed.

### make the sauce

Pour the 1 cup of the wine into a medium saucepan, set over medium heat, bring to a simmer, and simmer until reduced to ¼ cup, about 10 minutes. Add 2 cups of the Besciamella sauce, stir to mix, and continue to simmer until the mixture is warmed all the way through, about 1 minute. Turn off the heat, cover, and set aside until you're ready to serve.

### make the ravioli

Lightly dust three sheet pans with flour. Stack the four pasta sheets on one of the flour-dusted pans. In a small bowl, whisk the egg with 2 Tbsp water to make an egg wash.

Cut the pasta sheets into eight 6-inch squares. Transfer two pasta sheets to a second flour-dusted pan. Brush each pasta sheet lightly with the egg wash on one side. Scoop one-fourth of the mushroom filling onto the center of each pasta square. Top each one with a second pasta square.

Pushing from the center toward the edges with your fingers, remove any air bubbles and seal the dough, crimping along the edges. Dust both sides of the ravioli with flour. Transfer to the third flour-dusted pan. Repeat with the remaining pasta squares and filling to create four giant mushroom ravioli.

**CHEF PRO TIP:** You really need to force out as much of the air from each ravioli as possible. Start from the center and push the air out toward the pasta edge. This will keep them from popping when you boil them.

### boil the ravioli

In a 4 qt stockpot over medium-high heat, bring 3 qt salted water to a gentle boil. Carefully place one or two ravioli in the pot. (Don't try to cook more than one or two at a time, as you need the water to circulate freely.) The ravioli will sink, then float to the surface. Continue to cook for 30 seconds longer. The total cooking time should be 2 to 3 minutes. Do not overcook.

### assemble and serve

Using a large slotted spoon or skimmer, transfer each ravioli to a warmed individual bowl. Drizzle with a little olive oil and keep warm. Repeat until all four ravioli are cooked. Top each ravioli with the warm sauce and garnish with the reserved mushrooms and the basil. This is one humongous fungus of goodness. Pair your big ravioli with an equally big wine to dine like the Romans do!

### FARRO

1 Tbsp grapeseed or canola oil

1 cup semi-pearled or pearled farro

¼ tsp cumin seeds

3 cups vegetable stock, homemade (page 206) or purchased, or water

Pinch of kosher salt

### SQUASH AND GREEN ONIONS

1 delicata squash

1 Tbsp grapeseed or canola oil, plus more for brushing

Kosher salt and freshly ground black pepper

4 green onions, root ends trimmed

### CURRY

1 Tbsp grapeseed or canola oil

1 garlic clove, mashed to a paste

1 tsp finely grated, peeled fresh ginger

1 small shallot, minced

1 Tbsp tomato paste

2 tsp curry powder

2 tsp ground coriander

1 tsp ground cumin

¼ tsp ground turmeric

One 28-oz can diced fire-roasted tomatoes with juices

1½ cups dried French green lentils, rinsed

1 medium carrot, peeled and diced

½ cup diced red bell pepper

4 cups vegetable stock, homemade (page 206) or purchased, or water

½ tsp cayenne pepper (optional)

Pinch of kosher salt

16 green beans, trimmed and cut crosswise into thirds

½ cup diced zucchini

½ cup diced yellow squash

1 cup trimmed sugar snap peas

1 cup finely chopped fresh cilantro for garnish

# green lentil & veggie curry

This is a complex dish full of layered textures, rich flavors, and captivating aromas. It's a sensory overload (but in a good way). You don't often see a lot of delicata squash or charred onion in a curry dish, but the added texture and earthiness they deliver give this curry enough distinction to pair with one of our lighter white wines. The end result is a curry dish that's full of spices—not heat—and flavor that will keep you coming back for seconds.

## WINE PAIRING

*James Gang Reserve* Riesling

*Dream Weaver* Sparkling

**PREP TIME**
30 TO 40 MINUTES

**COOK TIME**
60 TO 90 MINUTES

**MAKES**
4 TO 6 SERVINGS

**VEG/VG**

### cook the farro

In a medium saucepan over medium heat, warm the oil for 1 minute. Add the farro and cumin, stir to coat the farro with the oil, and cook, stirring, to toast lightly, about 1 minute. Add the stock and salt and bring everything to a boil. Turn down the heat to low, cover, and simmer until all the liquid is absorbed and the farro is tender, about 30 minutes. Remove from the heat and keep warm.

### roast the squash and green onions

While the farro is simmering, roast the squash and green onions. Preheat the oven to 450°F. Cut the delicata squash in half lengthwise. Using a big spoon, scoop out and discard the seeds. Cut each half crosswise into ¼-inch-thick half-moons and transfer them to a medium bowl. Drizzle with the oil, season with salt and pepper, and toss to coat each piece.

Lay the squash pieces in a single layer on a sheet pan and roast until lightly browned, about 10 minutes. Remove from the oven and set aside.

Lay the green onions on a second sheet pan, brush with a little oil, and season with salt and pepper. Roast until the ends start to char, 4 to 5 minutes. Remove from the oven and set aside.

### make the curry

While the squash and green onions are roasting, make the curry. In a medium saucepan over medium-high heat, warm the oil. Add the garlic, ginger, and shallot and sauté for 1 minute.

Add the tomato paste, curry powder, coriander, cumin, and turmeric and cook, stirring, for 1 more minute. Add the tomatoes, lentils, carrot, and bell pepper and continue to cook and stir for 1 minute to coat everything with the spices.

Pour in the stock, add the cayenne (if using) and salt, and bring to a simmer. Turn down the heat to low and cook, uncovered, stirring occasionally, until the lentils are tender, 30 to 40 minutes.

**CHEF PRO TIP:** If too much of the liquid in the saucepan evaporates, you can always add a little more. You want the curry to stay "saucy" like a stew.

Once the lentils are tender, add the green beans, zucchini, yellow squash, and snap peas, stir well, and continue to simmer on low heat until the vegetables are tender, 4 to 5 minutes.

### assemble and serve

Fold the delicata squash pieces into the warm curry. To serve, scoop a generous portion of farro into each individual bowl and top with a ladle of the curry. Garnish each serving with the cilantro and a roasted green onion. Lovely!

# red wine risotto

Warm and inviting, well-made risotto is an ideal "one-pot dish" that's sure to satisfy even the toughest critics. The secret to truly great risotto is a little extra TLC at the stove and, of course, the right bottle of wine, like our *Silver Reserve* Lagrein, at the table.

### WINE PAIRING

*Silver Reserve* **Lagrein**

*Bella Bella* **Barbera**

*Primo* **Sangiovese**

3½ cups vegetable stock or chicken stock, homemade (page 206) or purchased

5 Tbsp unsalted butter

1 cup finely chopped yellow onion

2 garlic cloves, minced

1 cup Arborio rice

½ cup *Primo* Sangiovese

⅓ cup frozen green peas, thawed (optional)

¼ cup chopped fresh flat-leaf parsley leaves

½ cup grated Parmesan cheese, plus more for garnish

Kosher salt and freshly ground black pepper

2 Tbsp fresh goat cheese (optional)

In a small saucepan over medium-high heat, bring the stock to a simmer. Turn down the heat to low and cover to keep hot.

In a medium, heavy saucepan over medium heat, melt 3 Tbsp of the butter. Add the onion and cook, stirring often, until translucent and soft but not browned, about 8 minutes. Stir in the garlic and cook, stirring, for 30 seconds. Stir in the rice and cook, stirring often, until the rice is toasted, about 2 minutes. Finally, add the wine and stir until the wine is absorbed, 1 to 2 minutes.

Turn down the heat to medium-low, add ¾ cup of the hot stock, and simmer, stirring often, until the liquid is absorbed, 5 to 6 minutes. Add another ¾ cup of the hot stock and again simmer, stirring often, until it is absorbed, 5 to 6 minutes. Repeat in this manner until all the stock has been added.

**CHEF PRO TIP:** The secret to a creamy risotto is adding the stock in small portions (instead of all at once). When you add the stock in increments, the rice absorbs it gradually and releases some of the rice starch into the remaining liquid. It's all about pacing. Adding the stock in batches means a few extra steps, but the delicious result is worth it!

Once all the stock has been added and absorbed, test the rice for "doneness." Not all rice cooks the same. If the rice is still a little crunchy, add a little warm water and cook, stirring, until the rice softens.

When the risotto is ready, remove it from the heat and stir in the peas (if using), parsley, and the remaining 2 Tbsp butter. Then add the Parmesan and stir to combine. The risotto should have a porridge-like consistency—not too thin, not too thick.

Season the risotto with salt and pepper, then divide among four individual bowls, sprinkle with as much extra Parmesan cheese and goat cheese (if using) as you like, and serve.

**PREP TIME**
10 MINUTES

**COOK TIME**
30 TO 40 MINUTES

**MAKES**
4 SERVINGS

**GF/VEG**

I'M IN A RED WINE
STATE OF MIND

# the vineyard

In a vineyard, every season brings its own special reason to get excited. Behind the tasting room and winery, our vineyards are planted with Syrah, Cabernet Sauvignon, Cabernet Franc, Merlot, and Zinfandel grapes.

BUD BREAK

Pre-flowering calyptras

Veraison

Ripe and ready

OUR ESTATE VINEYARD

# pacific snapper with fresh peach salsa

**WINE PAIRING**

*Radiance*
Chardonnay

Pacific snapper is a light, mild fish, which is why it's the perfect protein to pair with this zesty salsa. It's also why it pairs so well with a crisp, fruit-forward white wine, like our *Radiance* Chardonnay. The flavor of this dish really comes from the salsa, so don't scrimp on the ingredients. We recommend using fresh, juicy peaches when they're in season (summer and early fall).

**PREP TIME**
30 TO 40 MINUTES

**COOK TIME**
15 TO 25 MINUTES

**MAKES**
4 SERVINGS

**GF**

**PEACH SALSA**

½ cup diced yellow peach

½ cup diced white peach

¼ cup diced red onion

¼ cup diced red bell pepper

2 Tbsp fresh lime juice

2 Tbsp extra-virgin olive oil

1 tsp honey

**PACIFIC SNAPPER**

Kosher salt and freshly ground black pepper

8 to 10 green beans, trimmed

8 to 10 yellow wax beans, trimmed

2 Tbsp grapeseed oil

Four 4 to 6 oz pieces skinless Pacific red snapper or rockfish fillet

3 Tbsp unsalted butter

1 cup loosely packed fresh basil leaves, for garnish

1 cup arugula or basil microgreens, for garnish (optional)

### make the peach salsa

Bring a pot filled with water to a boil over high heat. It should be large enough to cook all the green beans and wax beans at once. While you're waiting for the water to boil, you can make the peach salsa.

In a glass or stainless-steel bowl, combine the yellow and white peaches, onion, bell pepper, lime juice, olive oil, and honey and stir gently to mix well. Set aside until serving.

### cook the beans

Once the water comes to a boil, add salt. The water should taste like the ocean. Next, add the green beans and wax beans and boil for 4 to 8 minutes. The beans should be cooked but not soft. They should have a little crunch.

While the beans are cooking, fill a large bowl with ice water. Once the beans are done, drain them and immerse them in the ice water for about 5 minutes to chill. This will lock in the color and prevent them from overcooking. Don't worry, you'll reheat them later.

### cook the snapper

Heat a large cast-iron frying pan over medium-high heat. When the pan is hot, add the grapeseed oil. When the oil begins to smoke lightly, carefully add two pieces of the fish.

Cook until the fish is golden brown on the underside, 2 to 3 minutes. Flip the pieces over and add 1 Tbsp of the butter to the pan. Then, using a kitchen spoon, baste the fish with the now bubbling butter until the fish is cooked through, about 1 minute. Transfer the fish to a plate and keep warm. Repeat with the remaining two pieces of fish and 1 Tbsp of the butter.

**CHEF PRO TIP:** Once the fish is in the pan, don't move it! Let the crust develop. Flip it only once for perfectly seared fish fillets.

When all the fish is cooked, wipe out the pan, return it to the stove top over medium heat, and melt the remaining 1 Tbsp butter. Add the chilled beans and sauté until warmed through, 2 to 3 minutes. Season with salt and pepper and remove from the heat.

To serve, divide the beans among four individual plates and follow them with the fish fillets. Then add a generous spoonful of the salsa to each plate. Garnish with the basil and the arugula (if using) and raise a glass to one of the most vibrant and flavorful fish dishes you'll ever eat!

THIS DISH IS
A REAL PEACH!

DILL-LICIOUS!

# mustard-crusted black cod

Black cod is a naturally fatty fish, which means it won't dry out as easily as many other white fish. The Dijon mustard brings a kick of acidity to balance the more rounded flavors, adding up to an adventurous fish entrée that matches up beautifully with either a zesty white, like our *Sundance* Sauvignon Blanc, or a light-bodied red, like our *Tobin James* Pinot Noir.

**WINE PAIRING**

*Sundance*
Sauvignon Blanc

*Tobin James*
Pinot Noir

**PREP TIME**
30 TO 40 MINUTES

**COOK TIME**
20 TO 30 MINUTES

**MAKES**
4 SERVINGS

GF

## DILL MUSTARD SAUCE

2 Tbsp grapeseed oil

¼ cup diced yellow onion

1 cup *James Gang Reserve* **Chardonnay**

¼ cup raw cashews

1 cup chicken stock, homemade (page 206) or purchased

¼ cup Dijon mustard

Kosher salt and freshly ground black pepper

1 Tbsp chopped fresh dill

## BLACK COD

Four 4 to 6 oz pieces skinless black cod fillet

2 cups shelled green peas, cooked, or thawed frozen green peas

2 Tbsp extra-virgin olive oil

Kosher salt and freshly ground black pepper

1 cup loosely packed fresh dill fronds for garnish

4 finger limes (aka caviar lime), halved, for garnish (optional)

### make the dill mustard sauce

Make the sauce first since it's both the sauce *and* the marinade.

In a small saucepan over medium heat, warm 1 Tbsp of the grapeseed oil until it begins to smoke lightly. Add the onion and cook, stirring occasionally, until translucent, 2 to 3 minutes. Do not allow the onion to brown. Add the wine, bring to a simmer, and simmer until reduced by half, about 8 minutes.

Add the cashews and stock, turn down the heat to low, and simmer gently until the cashews are soft, 5 to 8 minutes. Remove from the heat and let cool for a minute or two. Transfer to a blender and blend on high speed until smooth, about 1 minute. Add the mustard and blend for another 30 seconds. Pour the sauce into a glass or stainless-steel bowl and season with salt and pepper. Cover and refrigerate for 10 to 15 minutes.

Once the sauce is cold, stir in the dill.

### make the black cod

Rub 2 Tbsp of the chilled mustard sauce on the fish pieces, coating them on both sides. This is gonna be a little messy, as you need to coat the fish thoroughly. Place the fish pieces on a plate and refrigerate for 30 minutes. Return the mustard sauce to the fridge at the same time.

While the fish is chilling, preheat the oven to 400°F. Rinse out the blender canister, return it

to the base, and add the peas and olive oil. Blend on high speed, adding water as needed (up to a few Tbsp) to make sure the blades "catch" on the peas, until the mixture is smooth, 30 to 60 seconds. Pour the pea purée into a small saucepan and season with salt and pepper. Set aside for now.

Line a sheet pan with parchment paper. Remove the fish from the fridge and arrange the pieces on the parchment-lined pan. Bake until the mustard marinade on the fish starts to brown lightly, 8 to 10 minutes. Remove from the oven.

**CHEF PRO TIP:** You can tell when cod is cooked by looking at the edges. The fillet will start to pull apart when it's done. Once you start to see a fillet "crack," immediately remove the fish from the oven.

To serve, warm the pea purée over medium heat until warm, 3 to 4 minutes. Divide the fish pieces among four individual plates and follow with a fancy smear of warm pea purée alongside the fish. Garnish the plates with the dill fronds. If using the finger limes, garnish each plate with the "pearls" squeezed from two lime halves. Finally, add a dollop of the chilled mustard sauce to each plate and toast your culinary success with a nice full glass of *Sundance* Sauvignon Blanc.

# petrale sole in parchment

Have you ever cooked with a paper oven? Now you can. With parchment paper you can create a mini steamer to cook delicate petrale sole, marrying it with the juices of the other ingredients to create a unique sauce. This dish is one of the coolest preparations in this entire book and at the winery. Watch the look on your guests' faces as they literally tear into this dish for a mouthwatering entrée that will leave them talking for months.

## WINE PAIRING

*Sundance* **Sauvignon Blanc**

*James Gang Reserve* **Chardonnay**

**PREP TIME**
20 TO 30 MINUTES

**COOK TIME**
15 TO 20 MINUTES

**MAKES**
4 SERVINGS

**GF**

2 Tbsp unsalted butter

1 large yellow onion, thinly sliced

Kosher salt and freshly ground black pepper

1 lemon

Four 5 oz pieces skinless petrale sole fillets

1 cup cherry tomatoes, halved

1 cup Castelvetrano olives, pitted and halved

¼ cup drained capers

Extra-virgin olive oil, for drizzling

Leaves from 1 bunch fresh basil

Preheat the oven to 450°F.

In a large sauté pan over medium heat, melt the butter. When the butter begins to bubble but not brown, add the onion slices and cook, stirring occasionally, until golden brown, 10 to 15 minutes. Remove from the heat and season with salt and pepper. Let cool to room temperature.

---

**CHEF PRO TIP:** Don't season a large amount of onions until after you cook them or you might over-season them. It's better to season them after they cook down.

---

Cut the lemon in half crosswise, then cut half of the lemon crosswise into thin wheels. Juice the other half of the lemon. Cut four pieces of parchment paper, each measuring 8 by 12 inches. Lay the parchment rectangles vertically on a work surface (see assembly and wrapping photos on pages 130–131).

For each packet, pile one-fourth of the caramelized onion on the bottom half of the parchment (the half nearest you). Season a piece of fish on both sides with salt and pepper and lay it on top of the onion. Place a wheel of lemon on top of the fish. Sprinkle one-fourth each of the tomatoes, olives, and capers on top of the lemon and fish, then drizzle with a little oil and one-fourth of the lemon juice. Top with one-fourth of the basil leaves.

Fold the top half of parchment over the bottom half to cover the onion, fish, and other ingredients. Starting at one corner, make a series of triangular folds around the open edges of the packet to seal in the fish and other ingredients. We usually make eight folds. Twist the ends to secure. You're essentially creating a closed envelope for all the ingredients. Repeat to make four packets total.

Arrange the packets on a sheet pan. Bake the packets for 10 minutes. Pierce the packet with a thin metal skewer and then touch the tip of the skewer to the back of your hand to see if it is hot. If not hot, bake an additional 2 minutes.

To serve, transfer the hot parchment packets to individual plates. For each packet, cut 2 large slits in the top of the packet, forming an X about 5 inches long. Be careful, as the steam is very hot! Garnish the interior with fresh basil and encourage your guests to literally tear into it.

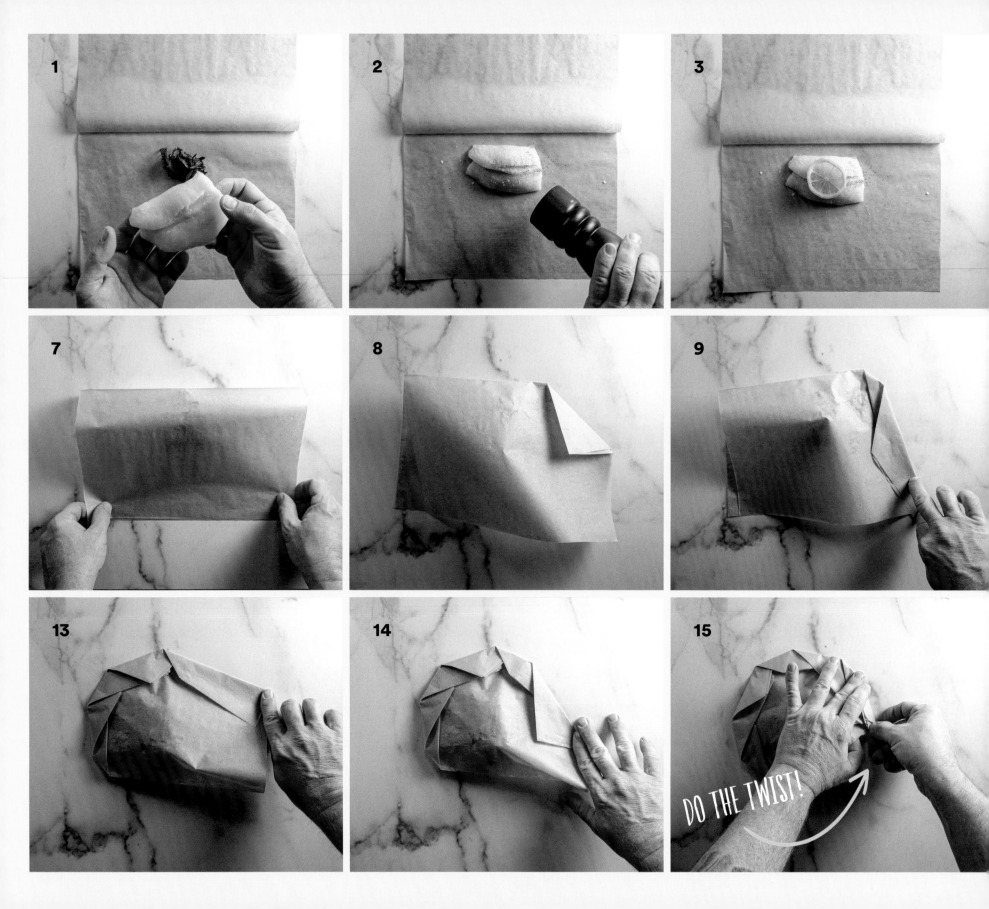

DO THE TWIST!

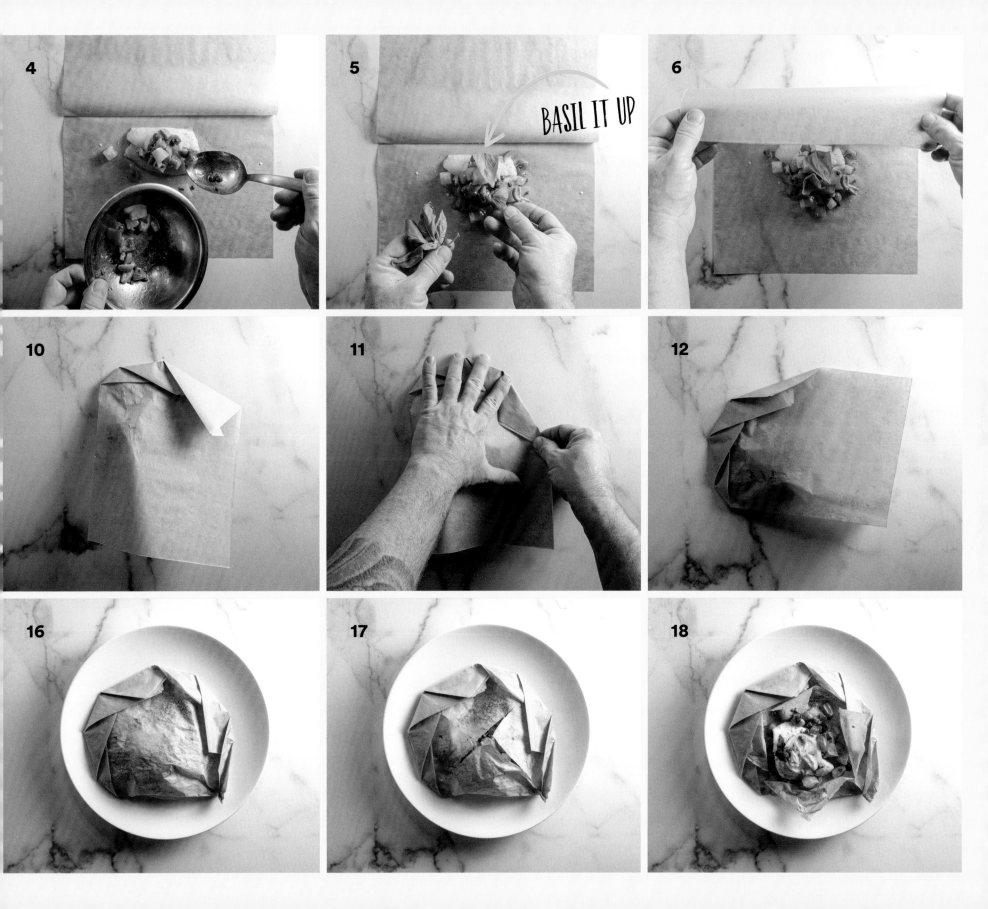

BASIL IT UP

### MARINATED SEA BASS

1 cup *Radiance* **Chardonnay**

¼ cup local or orange blossom honey

1 cup soy sauce

1 Tbsp red miso paste (in the refrigerated section in the market)

1 Tbsp molasses

Four 5 oz pieces skinless Chilean sea bass fillet

### BRAISED VEGETABLES

2 Tbsp toasted sesame oil

1 Tbsp minced garlic

1 Tbsp minced peeled fresh ginger

2 cups diced red bell pepper

2 cups snow peas or sugar snap peas, ends and strings removed

2 Tbsp chicken stock, homemade (page 206) or purchased

1 tsp soy sauce

1 tsp sesame seeds

½ cup sliced green onions, white and green parts

Kosher salt and freshly ground black pepper

Cumin Brown Rice (page 201) for serving

Sesame-Mustard Sauce (page 211) for serving

# miso-marinated sea bass with sesame-mustard sauce

### WINE PAIRING

*Radiance* Chardonnay

*Ballistic* Zinfandel

If you're looking for that "melt in your mouth" experience, this Chilean sea bass recipe is the ideal dish. Sea bass is packed with (good) fats and has a particularly smooth texture. Supercharge its already rich flavor with an equally bold marinade—and a dash of wine, of course!—for an entrée that holds a surprisingly complex mix of tastes and textures in a single bite. Sweet, lavish, and packed with layers of flavor, this Asian-inspired sea bass dish promises a nuanced wine-pairing experience that will change throughout your (hopefully) long and lovely meal with friends and family.

**PREP TIME**
30 MINUTES (PLUS 2 HOURS TO MARINATE)

**COOK TIME**
15 TO 20 MINUTES (PLUS 45 MINUTES FOR CUMIN BROWN RICE AND 10 MINUTES FOR SESAME-MUSTARD SAUCE)

**MAKES**
4 SERVINGS

**GF**

### marinate the sea bass

In a small saucepan over medium-high heat, combine the wine and honey and bring to a boil for about 5 minutes, or until all the alcohol has burned off. Remove from heat and stir in the soy sauce, miso, and molasses until dissolved. Transfer to a heatproof medium bowl, and let cool for a few minutes. Refrigerate until chilled, at least 15 minutes.

Put the fish pieces into the chilled marinade, immersing them, cover the bowl, and return it to the refrigerator for 2 hours. Be sure to flip each piece once at the halfway point (after 1 hour).

### make the braised vegetables

Preheat the oven to 500°F.

In a large sauté pan over medium-high heat, warm the oil. Add the garlic and ginger and sauté for 30 seconds (be careful not to burn the garlic!). Add the bell pepper and snow peas and continue to sauté for 1 minute. Then add the stock, soy sauce, sesame seeds, and green onions, turn down the heat to medium, and simmer until all the liquid is gone. This usually takes about 2 minutes. Remove from the heat and season with salt and pepper. Cover to keep warm.

### cook the sea bass

Oil a sheet pan (cooking spray is fine, too). Remove the fish from the marinade and place it on the prepared pan. Bake for about 10 minutes (or until the fish registers 130°F on an instant-read thermometer, if you have one handy). A perfectly cooked piece of sea bass should be a little dark around the edges.

**CHEF PRO TIP:** When choosing sea bass, you're looking for firm, bright white flesh. When cooking, the key to this dish is caramelizing the fish in the oven. If you can get the edges nice and dark, you've got a winner on your hands.

To serve, spoon the rice onto four individual plates. Top the rice with the fish and serve the braised vegetables alongside. Drizzle the fish and the plate with the sauce and serve.

# cedar plank salmon with red wine sauce

Cooking on a cedar plank might *sound* complicated, but the beauty of this dish is how easy it is. No, really. For truly great cedar plank salmon, all you need is fresh-caught salmon, a little red wine (or a lot!), some cedar planks, and a grill. Cooking fish on the grill this way locks in moisture, with most of the rich, smoky flavor coming from the fish gently smoking on the cedar. So start with fresh ingredients, keep an eye on the grill, and wow everyone with your red wine reduction sauce. Just make sure to distract your guests with a bottle of wine so they don't learn all your culinary secrets.

**SALMON**

Four 5 oz pieces skinless salmon fillets

Kosher salt and freshly ground black pepper

**SIDES**

2 Tbsp unsalted butter

2 cups thinly sliced leeks, white parts only

Kosher salt and freshly ground black pepper

8 oz green beans, trimmed

1½ tsp whole-grain mustard

**RED WINE SAUCE**

2 cup *RED* Blend

1 tsp Dijon mustard

¼ tsp sugar

2 fresh thyme sprigs

1 bay leaf

2 Tbsp unsalted butter, cut into 3 or 4 chunks

### prep the salmon

Soak four 6- by 3-inch cedar planks in water for at least 2 hours before cooking. Take the salmon out of the fridge 15 minutes before cooking, while you make the sides and sauce.

### make the sides

In a medium, heavy sauté pan over medium heat, melt the butter. Add the leeks, turn down the heat to low, and cook, stirring occasionally, until the leeks start to break down and become soft and pliable, 5 to 10 minutes. Season with salt and pepper and remove from the heat. Cover to keep warm and set aside until serving.

In a medium saucepan over high heat, bring 8 cups water to a boil. Add 1 Tbsp salt and then add the beans. Boil for 4 to 8 minutes. The beans should be cooked but not soft. They should have a little crunch. Drain and season with salt and pepper. Cover to keep warm and set aside until serving.

### make the sauce

In a medium, heavy saucepan over medium heat, combine the wine, Dijon mustard, sugar, thyme, and bay leaf and bring to a simmer, stirring to mix well. Simmer until reduced to about 1 cup, 10 to 15 minutes. Remove and discard the thyme and bay leaf.

Turn down the heat to low and add the butter, a chunk at a time, whisking after each addition until the butter melts. This will create an emulsion. You can also use an immersion blender to mix in the butter. Remove from the heat.

### grill the salmon

Fire up the grill for direct grilling over medium-high heat. Season each salmon piece on both sides with salt and pepper and set each piece directly on a cedar plank. Place the cedar planks on the cooking grate and close the grill lid. If you like, cap the salmon on the grill with an upside-down 2-inch-deep pan to trap more of the smoke (and flavor). You can also use a metal bowl. No cap is necessary, however.

Cook the salmon to an internal temperature of between 128°F and 132°F or to your preferred "doneness": medium rare is 128°F, about 8 minutes; medium is 132°F, about 12 minutes; and well done is 140°F, about 15 minutes.

You want the cedar planks to smoke a bit, but make sure they *don't* catch on fire! Small salmon pieces cook more quickly than larger pieces, so keep an eye on the grill.

---

CHEF PRO TIP: Keep a spray bottle of water by your side. If the cedar catches fire, give it a little squirt. Just try not to spray the fish.

---

To serve, divide the leeks and green beans among four individual plates and top with the salmon pieces and whole-grain mustard. Then drizzle the red wine sauce on the plate for an elegant backyard barbecue masterpiece. Keep the cedar planks as a trophy.

## WINE PAIRING

*Tobin James*
**Pinot Noir**

*Primo*
**Sangiovese**

*RED* **Blend**

**PREP TIME**
20 MINUTES (PLUS
2 HOURS TO SOAK PLANKS)

**COOK TIME**
30 TO 35 MINUTES

**MAKES**
4 SERVINGS

**GF**

6 Tbsp grapeseed oil

½ cup diced yellow onion

3 cups cauliflower florets

1 Tbsp extra-virgin olive oil

4 garlic cloves

½ cup raw cashews

Kosher salt and ground white pepper

2 baby eggplants, each about 5 oz

8 large diver sea scallops (U/10), preferably dry-packed, "foot" removed

2 Tbsp curry powder

8 broccolini

1 tsp chat masala or ground coriander for garnish

1 cup microgreens, such as bull's blood beet and/or arugula, for garnish

CHAT MASALA

# cast-iron diver sea scallops

WINE PAIRING

*Radiance*
Chardonnay

---

**PREP TIME**
20 TO 30 MINUTES

**COOK TIME**
30 TO 45 MINUTES

**MAKES**
4 SERVINGS

**GF**

Diver sea scallops are some of the meatiest and most flavorful seafood you can get. And that's because true "diver" scallops are harvested by scuba divers. The best way to cook this hand-picked delicacy is in a cast-iron pan to create a delicious crust that locks in the rich and meaty flavors. When seared correctly, the brininess of fresh scallops balances perfectly with the creaminess of the cauliflower purée and roasted eggplant for a fusion of crunchy texture and smooth flavor. Pair this dish with our clean, bright unoaked *Radiance* Chardonnay for a lighter wine-focused meal that lets you revel in each and every bite.

## make the sides

In a medium saucepan over medium heat, warm 1 Tbsp of the grapeseed oil. Add the onion and cook, stirring often, until translucent, 2 to 3 minutes. Make sure the onion does not take on any color. This is one of the few times you *don't* want golden brown onions!

Add the cauliflower, olive oil, and garlic cloves and cook, stirring occasionally, until the cauliflower begins to soften, about 2 minutes. Add the cashews and just enough water to cover everything and bring to a simmer. Turn down the heat to low and simmer gently until the cauliflower softens, 5 to 10 minutes. Remove from the heat.

Using a slotted spoon, transfer all the solids in the pan to a blender. With the blender on medium speed, slowly add just enough cooking liquid from the pan for the blender blades to "catch" on the solids, then increase the speed to high and continue to blend until smooth and creamy, 1 to 2 minutes. Season with salt and white pepper.

Cut each eggplant in half lengthwise. Dust each cut side with salt. Set aside for 5 to 10 minutes until water droplets form on the cut surface.

Heat a large cast-iron frying pan over high heat. When the pan is hot, blot any moisture on the eggplants. Then add 2 Tbsp of the grapeseed oil to the hot pan. When the oil is hot, add the eggplant halves, cut side down, and sear the eggplant until the cut sides are golden brown, 2 to 3 minutes. Flip the halves and cook until browned on the second side, 2 to 3 more minutes. Remove from the heat and transfer the eggplants to a plate. Keep warm.

## cook the scallops

Wipe out the cast-iron pan and return it to high heat. Add 2 Tbsp of the grapeseed oil. While the oil is heating, in a medium bowl, toss the scallops with the curry powder and a pinch of salt, coating each scallop completely.

Add the scallops to the hot oil (all eight should fit in the pan at once) and sear until a solid crust forms on the bottom of each scallop. This usually takes 3 to 4 minutes. Flip and cook for another 2 minutes. Turn off the heat and let the scallops sit in the pan on the stove for 1 more minute.

---

**CHEF PRO TIP:** The key to seared scallops is a good cast-iron pan. It holds the heat, which helps develop a nice, even crust on the outside of the scallops

---

Transfer the scallops to a plate and keep warm. Add the remaining 1 Tbsp grapeseed oil and the broccolini to the pan, toss the broccolini with the oil and the fat left in the pan, and then cook over medium heat, stirring occasionally, until lightly charred, 3 to 4 minutes.

Place two scallops, an eggplant half, one-fourth of the broccolini, a large smear of cauliflower-cashew puree, and a dusting of chat masala on each plate, then finish the plates with the microgreens to make them look (and taste) extra nice.

# *TᴺT* grilled smoky shrimp

This dish is all about the marinade. Once you add fresh super colossal shrimp—labeled "U-12," which means twelve shrimp per pound—to the blend of smoked paprika and *Urfa biber* (that's a delicious smoky Turkish chile), you're in for a smoky, fiery, fun shrimp dish with flavor that lingers. Served with saffron-infused Spanish rice, these shrimp are a BBQ aficionado's dream come true and pair beautifully with our complex and luxurious *TᴺT* Tannat/Tempranillo Blend. To save time and cleanup, use part of the grill to cook up a batch of grilled vegetables along with the shrimp.

### SPANISH RICE

2 Tbsp grapeseed oil

½ cup diced yellow onion

½ cup diced carrot

1 Tbsp minced garlic

¼ tsp saffron threads

½ tsp fresh thyme leaves

1 cup short-grain brown rice

2 cups chicken or vegetable stock, homemade (page 206) or purchased

½ cup tomato sauce

½ cup *TᴺT* Tannat/Tempranillo Blend

½ cup shelled fresh green peas, cooked, or thawed frozen green peas

### GARLIC SAUCE

2 Tbsp grapeseed oil

½ cup chopped yellow onion

¼ cup minced garlic

1 Tbsp tomato paste

2 Tbsp chicken or vegetable stock, homemade (page 206) or purchased

### SHRIMP MARINADE

1 Tbsp smoked paprika

1 Tbsp Hungarian sweet paprika

1 tsp garlic powder

1 tsp onion powder

1 tsp kosher salt

1 tsp *Urfa biber* (chile) powder or other chile powder (optional)

½ cup extra-virgin olive oil

1 Tbsp fresh lemon juice

12 super colossal shrimp (U-12), peeled and deveined

### make the rice

In a medium saucepan over medium-high heat, warm the grapeseed oil until it begins to smoke lightly. Add the onion, carrot, and garlic and sauté for 1 minute. Add the saffron and thyme and continue to sauté for 30 seconds. Add the rice and stir to coat thoroughly with the oil and vegetables. Then add the stock, tomato sauce, and wine, stir well, and bring to a simmer.

Cover, turn down the heat to low, and cook until all the liquid is absorbed and the rice is tender, about 30 minutes. When the rice is cooked, remove from the heat, fold in the peas, re-cover, and set aside until serving.

### make the sauce

In a medium sauté pan over medium-high heat, warm the grapeseed oil. Add the onion and garlic and sauté lightly for 1 minute, making sure the garlic does not burn. The onion and garlic should be translucent and softened. Turn down the heat to low and fold in the tomato paste. Add the stock, bring to a simmer, and simmer for 1 minute. Remove from the heat and keep warm until serving.

### make the marinade

In a medium glass or stainless-steel bowl, whisk together both paprikas, the garlic and onion powders, salt, *Urfa biber* (if using), olive oil, and lemon juice. Let sit for 5 minutes. Add the shrimp to the bowl and stir to coat evenly. Let sit for an additional 5 minutes. (The shrimp can sit in the marinade for up to 30 minutes but no more or the salt starts to "cook" the shrimp.)

**CHEF PRO TIP:** Before you put the shrimp on the grill, be sure to shake off the excess marinade. Too much oil can make the fire flare up.

### grill the shrimp

Fire up the grill for direct grilling over high heat. Time to put the shrimp on the barbie. Arrange them on the cooking grate directly over the fire and grill, turning once, until nicely charred and cooked through, 3 to 4 minutes on each side. The key to crispy, charred shrimp with a tender center is high heat.

To serve, divide the shrimp and rice among four individual plates, then top the shrimp with the warm garlic sauce. Get ready for a dynamite dinner!

WINE PAIRING

*Sundance*
Sauvignon Blanc

*Tobin James*
Pinot Noir

*TnT* Tannat/
Tempranillo Blend

PREP TIME
30 TO 40 MINUTES

COOK TIME
30 TO 45 MINUTES

MAKES
4 SERVINGS

GF

# the crush

Once our grapes reach the perfect maturity and ripeness, the real fun begins! Harvest and crush are always exciting and hectic—working seven days a week at the mercy of the grapes. Making great wine is worth all the late hours and early mornings, especially when you get to enjoy the *fruits* of your labor.

COMING SOON TO A BOTTLE NEAR YOU!

A LANCE FAVORITE

### MARINADE

½ cup extra-virgin olive oil

½ cup sliced green onions, white and green parts

12 fresh sage leaves

½ cup loosely packed fresh rosemary leaves

1 tsp smoked paprika

Kosher salt and freshly ground black pepper

### CHICKEN

One 3 to 4 lb chicken, de-boned without breaking the skin (ask your butcher to do it), or 4 boneless, skin-on chicken breasts

1 Tbsp grapeseed oil

### DIJON SAUCE

1 cup cauliflower florets

½ cup chopped yellow onion

6 garlic cloves, chopped

1½ cups chicken stock, homemade (page 206) or purchased

2 Tbsp Dijon mustard

Kosher salt and freshly ground black pepper

# brick chicken

If you've never turned a chicken inside out, you will now! Roll up your sleeves because you're literally going to marinate the inside of a bird for this one-of-a-kind chicken recipe. It's a great way to cook chicken quickly without it drying out. The pressure of the "brick" compacts the meat so the heat reaches the middle right away without sucking the moisture (and flavor) out of the bird. It cuts the cooking time in half, which gives you more time to drink wine! Pair this old Italian-style favorite with our buttery *James Gang Reserve* Chardonnay or a robust red, like the *Silver Reserve* Merlot, and turn your taste buds inside out!

## WINE PAIRING

*James Gang Reserve* **Chardonnay**

*Silver Reserve* **Merlot**

**PREP TIME**
15 TO 20 MINUTES (PLUS 30 TO 40 MINUTES TO MARINATE)

**COOK TIME**
25 TO 30 MINUTES

**MAKES**
4 SERVINGS

**GF**

### make the marinade

Put the olive oil in the blender first, followed by the green onions, sage, rosemary, and paprika. Blend on high speed for 1 minute. You want a thin paste. Pour the paste into a large bowl and season with salt and pepper.

### marinate the chicken

If you're able to get a deboned chicken, turn it inside out so the meat is on the outside and the skin is inside. Rub the marinade you have just made all over the meat. Then turn the chicken skin side out and let it rest in the refrigerator for 30 to 40 minutes while you make the Dijon sauce. If you're using boneless chicken breasts, rub the marinade all over the chicken breasts in the marinade bowl; cover and let rest in the refrigerator. Make the sauce while the chicken marinates.

### make the dijon sauce

In a medium saucepan over medium heat, combine the cauliflower, onion, garlic, and stock and bring to a simmer. Cover and simmer until the cauliflower falls apart, 5 to 10 minutes.

Remove from the heat and let cool for a minute or two, then transfer the contents of the pan to a blender. Add the mustard and blend on high speed until smooth, about 1 minute. You don't want any chunks. If the sauce is too thick, thin it with a little water and blend briefly to mix. Pour the sauce into a bowl and set it aside.

### cook the chicken

In a 12-inch cast-iron frying pan over medium heat, warm the grapeseed oil until it begins to smoke lightly. Add the chicken, breast side down, and place a second 12-inch cast-iron pan on top of the chicken, creating some pressure. Cook, turning once, for 10 minutes on each side.

The finished chicken should be golden brown on both sides and an instant-read thermometer inserted into the thickest part of the meat should register at least 160°F. The size of the bird will affect the cook time. This recipe calls for a whole bird weighing 3 to 4 lb, so if you can only find a smaller bird or you are using chicken breasts, you'll need to adjust your cook time down.

**CHEF PRO TIP:** If you don't have two cast-iron pans, you can wrap a brick in aluminum foil and set it on the chicken. That's why it's called "brick chicken." You just need something heavy enough to press the meat into the pan. CHEF PRO TIP within a Pro Tip: Don't use a dirty brick!

To serve, cut the chicken into crosswise slices. Divide the chicken between four individual plates and top with a generous dollop of Dijon sauce.

# leduc's lemon roasted chicken

There's nothing more comforting than a freshly roasted chicken, especially when it has been rubbed with your very own homemade herb butter. That's right, you're going to make a simple yet flavorful rub—from scratch—and it's going to taste even better than you imagined. And the best part is that you can pair the finished dish with nearly every single wine we make. This chicken will "dance with just about anyone." The secret to preparing a great bird is to highlight its natural juiciness with just the right mix of zest and spice. Luckily, we've got just the right mix for you. Follow along and you'll create a perfectly roasted chicken that will get your friends and family talking about you. But be warned, once people taste this dish, you might have to make your "mind-blowing" chicken again and again to satisfy the crowds lining up outside your house.

## WINE PAIRING

*James Gang Reserve* **Chardonnay**

*Chateau Le Cacheflo*

*Notorious* **Cabernet Sauvignon**

*James Gang Reserve* **Primitivo**

**PREP TIME**
40 TO 50 MINUTES

**COOK TIME**
50 TO 60 MINUTES

**MAKES**
4 SERVINGS

**GF**

### GARLIC MUSTARD SAUCE

10 garlic cloves

1 cup extra-virgin olive oil

1½ Tbsp stone-ground mustard

1 Tbsp fresh lemon juice

1 Tbsp chopped fresh flat-leaf parsley leaves

Kosher salt and freshly ground black pepper

### CHICKEN

2 Tbsp unsalted butter, at room temperature

5 garlic cloves, minced

½ tsp minced fresh thyme

½ tsp minced fresh rosemary

1 Tbsp chopped fresh flat-leaf parsley leaves

3 lemons

Kosher salt and freshly ground black pepper

One 4 lb whole chicken

### ARTICHOKES

2 artichokes

Extra-virgin olive oil, for brushing

Kosher salt and freshly ground black pepper

### make the sauce

In a small saucepan over medium heat, combine the garlic and oil and cook for 10 to 15 minutes. The garlic cloves are ready when they are slightly browned and soft. Do not allow them to brown too much or they will turn bitter. Remove the pan from the heat, scoop the garlic out of the oil, and chop it as finely as you can. In a small bowl, combine the chopped garlic and ½ cup of the cooking oil and refrigerate until chilled, 10 to 15 minutes. Reserve the remaining ½ cup oil for another use.

Add the mustard, lemon juice, and parsley to the chilled garlic-oil mixture, season with salt and pepper, and whisk until well blended. The sauce is pretty thick, but you can easily thin it with a little water if you like. Set aside until serving.

### roast the chicken

Position a rack in the lower third of the oven and preheat the oven to 425°F. This puts the chicken right smack in the middle of the oven, which will help the bird cook evenly and give the skin a nice crisp finish.

In a small bowl, mix together the butter, garlic, thyme, rosemary, and parsley. Finely grate ½ tsp zest from 1 lemon and mix the zest into the butter mixture. Halve the zested lemon, and set the halves aside. Season the butter mixture with salt and pepper. This is the herb butter that you'll be using to season your chicken, so make sure you like it!

*(recipe continues)*

THIS DISH IS SUPER
WINE FRIENDLY!

Next, pat the chicken dry with paper towels. Starting at the cavity, slip your fingers between the meat and skin to loosen the skin covering the breast, thighs, and drumsticks, being careful not to tear the skin. Then slide about half of the herb butter under the loosened skin and spread it evenly over the meat. Rub the remaining butter over the outside of the chicken. Season the cavity and the outside of the bird with salt and pepper. Place the reserved lemon halves inside the cavity. Truss the legs together with kitchen twine (if you have it).

Place the chicken, breast side up, in a roasting pan. Roast for 20 minutes, then rotate the pan 180 degrees halfway through cooking (so it cooks evenly) and continue to cook until an instant-read thermometer registers 165°F, about 20 minutes longer. Remove from the oven and let rest for 15 minutes.

**CHEF PRO TIP:** The best way to take the temperature of a chicken is to insert the thermometer into the inner thigh away from bone.

### grill the artichokes

While the chicken is roasting, fire up the grill for direct grilling over medium heat. Bring a medium saucepan filled with lightly salted water to a boil over high heat, add the artichokes, and boil for 15 to 20 minutes. You'll know they are ready when you can easily pull off one of the leaves. Drain the artichokes and let cool until they can be handled.

Cut each artichoke in half lengthwise. Scrape out the fuzzy "choke" center and pull off any prickly purple-tipped leaves. Lightly trim the stem and peel if woody. Brush the cut side of each artichoke half with oil and then season the cut sides with salt and pepper. Halve the remaining 2 lemons.

Place the artichoke halves, cut side down, on the cooking grate directly over the fire and cook, turning as needed, until lightly charred in spots and tender when pierced with a knife tip, about 10 minutes. When the artichokes are nearly finished, add the remaining 4 lemon halves and lightly grill to accompany your materpiece. People always like an extra bit of lemon.

To serve, carve the chicken. Divide between 4 individual plates. Finish each plate with an artichoke half, a lemon half, and a drizzle of garlic mustard sauce on the plate and artichoke. Serve with *James Gang Reserve* **Chardonnay** or your favorite Tobin James wine.

# red wine–braised chicken

Chicken braised in red wine, or *coq au vin*, is a classic French dish from Burgundy. But don't be intimidated by its origin. Like most traditional French dishes, all you need is a good bottle of wine and a handful of quality ingredients. Luckily, you have a few bottles of Tobin James, so you're off to a great start. Ask any French chef and they will tell you to use **Pinot Noir** for this recipe. We do. But honestly, you can (and should!) grab any great bottle of red off your shelf and experiment. Roll up your sleeves, grab your fanciest apron, crank up the *Amélie* soundtrack, and get ready to embrace your inner Julia Child. This standard of the French kitchen is a true wine lover's recipe. *C'est magnifique!*

## WINE PAIRING

*GSM* Blend

*Tobin James* Pinot Noir

*Made in the Shade* Merlot

**PREP TIME**
15 TO 20 MINUTES
(PLUS AT LEAST 2 HOURS
TO MARINATE)

**COOK TIME**
1 HOUR

**MAKES**
4 SERVINGS

4 boneless, skinless chicken thighs, each about 3 oz

2 boneless, skinless chicken breasts, each about 5 oz

1½ cups red wine, such as **Tobin James** Pinot Noir or **Made in the Shade** Merlot

1 cup chicken stock, homemade (page 206) or purchased

3 slices bacon, cut into ½-inch pieces

2 cups diced yellow onions

2 cups coarsely cut peeled carrots, in 1-inch pieces

4 garlic cloves, minced

2 Tbsp tomato paste

2 Tbsp fresh thyme leaves

8 oz cremini or button mushrooms, sliced

2 Tbsp unsalted butter, cut into small chunks

¼ cup all-purpose flour

Kosher salt and freshly ground black pepper

## marinate the chicken

In a medium glass or stainless-steel bowl, combine the chicken, wine, and stock and mix well. Cover and marinate in the refrigerator for at least 2 hours, though you can leave it overnight if you have the time. While you're at it, pour yourself a glass of **Tobin James** Pinot Noir so you can marinate a little too.

## cook the chicken

In a Dutch oven or other large, heavy pot over medium heat, cook the bacon until crispy, about 8 minutes. Remove from the heat and, using a slotted spoon, transfer the bacon to a plate lined with a paper towel. Leave the fat in the pot.

CHEF PRO TIP #1: When you cook with bacon, it's important not to season anything until the recipe is finished. The bacon adds a lot of salt to a dish, so you don't want to "pre-salt" too much. The same goes for reducing a sauce. If you season it before you evaporate the liquid, it may turn out too salty.

Remove the chicken pieces from the marinade (save the marinade for later!) and pat them dry. Return the pot to medium heat. When the bacon fat is hot, add the chicken pieces and cook, turning as needed, until golden brown on both sides, about 5 minutes on each side. You may have to brown the pieces in batches so you don't crowd the pan. As the pieces are browned, transfer them to a plate. Pour all but 2 Tbsp of the bacon and chicken fat into a small heatproof dish and set aside.

Return the pot to medium heat, add the onions and carrots, and cook, stirring occasionally, until golden brown, 8 to 10 minutes. Add the garlic and cook for 1 more minute.

Push the vegetables to one side of the pot, add the tomato paste to the empty side, and cook, stirring often, until the tomato paste starts to brown, 2 to 3 minutes. Add the wine and reserved marinade and use a wooden spoon to scrape up any bits stuck to the bottom of the pan. This is called "deglazing."

*(recipe continues)*

Bring to a simmer and then turn down the heat to low. Add the chicken pieces and thyme, cover the pot, and simmer until cooked through, about 20 minutes.

While the chicken is simmering, it's time to cook the mushrooms. In a medium frying pan over medium-high heat, warm 1 Tbsp of the reserved bacon and chicken fat. When the fat is hot, add the mushrooms and cook, stirring often, until golden brown, about 10 minutes. Transfer the mushrooms to the pot with the simmering chicken.

In a small bowl, combine the butter and flour and mix lightly to coat the butter with the flour. Then slowly add *just* the flour-coated butter slices, a piece at a time, to the simmering sauce and cook, stirring, until the butter melts and the sauce begins to thicken, about 2 minutes. Season with salt and pepper.

To serve, transfer to a serving bowl (or leave in the pot for family style), garnish with the cooked bacon, and enjoy!

RED WINE-BRAISED
CHICKEN

# roasted chicken tikka masala

This Indian-inspired dish is more flavorful and creamy than spicy and hot. Think elegance and flavor, not heat. A favorite of Lance and Claire, these skewers pair surprisingly well with lighter white wines, like our *Sundance* Sauvignon Blanc. You can even raise a glass of bubbly *Dream Weaver* Sparkling and toast one of the inspirations for this dish, the great chef Floyd Cardoz.

**WINE PAIRING**

*Sundance*
Sauvignon Blanc

*Dream Weaver*
Sparkling

**PREP TIME**
20 TO 30 MINUTES (PLUS 2 HOURS TO MARINATE)

**COOK TIME**
35 TO 40 MINUTES

**MAKES**
4 SERVINGS

GF

## MARINADE

1 cup plain full-fat Greek yogurt

3 Tbsp grapeseed oil

2 Tbsp fresh lemon juice

2 Tbsp ground cumin

2 tsp freshly ground black pepper

3 Tbsp sweet Hungarian paprika

1 tsp ground cinnamon

1 tsp kosher salt

One 2-inch piece fresh ginger, peeled and minced

4 boneless, skinless chicken breasts, each about 5 inches, cut into 1-inch cubes

## MASALA SAUCE

1 Tbsp unsalted butter

2 garlic cloves, minced

1 tsp minced peeled fresh ginger

½ jalapeño chile, minced

2 tsp ground coriander

1 tsp ground cumin

1 tsp smoked paprika

1 tsp garam masala

½ tsp kosher salt

One 28-oz can diced fire-roasted tomatoes with juices

1 cup heavy cream or plain full-fat yogurt

¼ cup chopped fresh cilantro

8 sprigs fresh cilantro for garnish

Cilantro-Mint Chutney (page 209) for serving

Steamed basmati rice for serving

Naan or pita bread, warmed, for serving

### make the marinade

In a blender, combine the yogurt, oil, lemon juice, cumin, black pepper, sweet Hungarian paprika, cinnamon, salt, and ginger and blend on high speed until smooth, about 1 minute. Place the chicken in a medium bowl and pour the marinade over the chicken, turning to coat evenly. Cover and marinate in the refrigerator for at least 2 hours or up to 24 hours.

About 1 hour before you are ready to roast the chicken, begin soaking four bamboo skewers in water (so they don't burn). About 20 minutes before you are ready to roast the chicken, preheat the oven to 500°F. While the chicken marinates, make the masala sauce.

### make the masala sauce

In a medium saucepan over medium heat, melt the butter. Add the garlic, ginger, and jalapeño and cook, stirring often, for 1 minute. Stir in the coriander, cumin, paprika, garam masala, salt, and tomatoes, turn down the heat to low, and simmer for 15 minutes to blend the flavors. Gently stir in the cream or yogurt and continue to simmer over low heat for 5 more minutes to heat through and blend well. Remove from the heat and stir in the cilantro. Keep warm.

### roast the chicken

Thread the chicken onto the soaked skewers (one breast per skewer) and arrange on a small sheet pan. Roast the chicken, turning the skewers occasionally to cook evenly, until cooked through, 12 to 15 minutes. There will be some dark spots on the chicken from the marinade browning. That's a good thing.

Transfer the skewers to a serving platter or individual plates, top the chicken with a generous amount of masala sauce (about ½ cup per skewer), and garnish with the cilantro sprigs. Serve with the chutney, rice, and naan.

# bacon pork tenderloin "roulade"

Wrapping the bacon around the pork ensures that every bite is gonna have the "porkiness" of the tenderloin and the natural salt and smokiness of the bacon. You might be wondering, "Isn't that too much pork?" No. There's no such thing. The natural sweetness of figs balances out the earthy richness of the pork for a concentrated burst of flavor in each bite that begs for a bold red wine, like our *GSM* Blend. Serve this pork-forward dish with seasonal vegetables like grilled zucchini or steamed spaghetti squash.

## WINE PAIRING

*GSM* Blend

*Fat Boy Zinfandel*

*Dusi Vineyard Zinfandel*

## TENDERLOINS

Two 12 to 16 oz pork tenderloins

Kosher salt and freshly ground black pepper

2 Tbsp grapeseed oil

12 slices hickory-smoked bacon

## FIG SAUCE

1 cup *GSM* Blend

1 cup veal demi-glace, homemade (page 208) or purchased

1 Tbsp Dijon mustard

Kosher salt and freshly ground black pepper

6 fresh figs, stemmed and diced

1 Tbsp chopped fresh basil

### sear the tenderloins

Trim all the excess fat and silverskin from the pork tenderloins. Silverskin is a fine layer of tough tissue between the fat and the meat. You don't want it. Fortunately, it is easy to remove. Working at the end of a tenderloin, slip the tip of a sharp knife under the silverskin, loosening enough of it from the meat to grab firmly with your fingers, then just pull it away from the meat. (It can be slippery, so you may want to grab it with a paper towel.) Season the meat with salt and pepper.

In a large cast-iron frying pan over medium-high heat, warm the oil until it begins to smoke lightly. Add the tenderloins and sear, turning as needed, until a nice brown crust forms on all sides, about 5 minutes. Transfer to a plate and let cool for 5 minutes.

**CHEF PRO TIP:** It's always better to sear meat in a hot cast-iron pan. The heavy pan holds heat better than a regular pan, which means you get a golden brown and delicious crust every time.

### wrap the tenderloins with bacon

While the meat is cooling, preheat the oven to 400°F. Lay out a 20-inch-long piece of plastic wrap and "shingle" half of the bacon slices lengthwise on the plastic wrap, overlapping each slice ¼ inch (photo 1).

Place one pork tenderloin at the bottom of the bacon slices (picture 2) and roll it up inside the bacon like a pig in a blanket (photo 3). Use the plastic wrap to help you roll the pork in the bacon. Grab both ends of the plastic wrap and roll the plastic forward (photos 4 and 5) like an old-fashioned toffee wrapper, then tie off each end with a knot or butcher's twine to keep the roll as tight to the meat as possible (photo 6).

Repeat with the second tenderloin and the remaining bacon. Chill the rolls in the refrigerator for 1 hour before you roast them.

*(recipe continues)*

**PREP TIME**

20 TO 25 MINUTES (PLUS 1 HOUR TO CHILL)

**COOK TIME**

40 TO 50 MINUTES

**MAKES**

4 TO 6 SERVINGS

GF

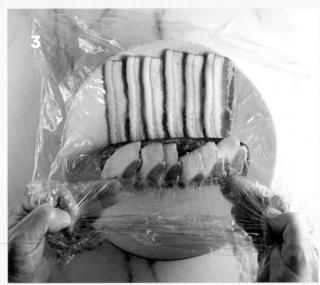

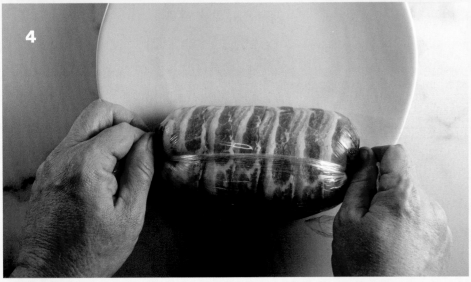

READY TO CHILL

### roast the tenderloins

Just before the rolls have finished chilling, preheat the oven to 400°F. Remove the rolls from the refrigerator and gently remove the plastic wrap (photo 7). Place the pork rolls on a sheet pan and season them with pepper on all sides, turning them gently. Then position the rolls seam side down to hold the bacon in place. You can also use toothpicks to hold the bacon on the pork, but the weight of the pork on the seam should keep the bacon from falling off.

Roast the tenderloins until the bacon is golden brown and an instant-read thermometer inserted into the center of each roll registers 150°F, 25 to 30 minutes. Remove from the oven and let rest for 8 to 10 minutes. While the pork rests, make the fig sauce.

### make the fig sauce

In a small saucepan over medium-high heat, bring the wine to a simmer and simmer until reduced to ¼ cup. This should take 8 to 10 minutes.

Turn down the heat to medium, add the demi-glace, and bring to a simmer. Whisk in the mustard and simmer for 1 minute. Remove from the heat and season with salt and pepper. Fold in the figs and basil and you're all set.

To serve, slice the tenderloins into 1-inch-thick slices. Place a spoonful of the sauce on each individual plate and top with the pork slices. And make sure you pour everyone a glass of that open bottle of *GSM* Blend!

# bone-in double pork chop

The only thing better than pork chops is *double* pork chops (with a glass of wine, of course). Everything about this recipe is double-strength—including the cooking methods. Roasted to preserve every drop of rich, natural, juicy flavor and grilled for that fiery kick of taste and color, this double pork chop is one of a kind. Plus, it is served with a sharp yet creamy mustard sauce that pairs beautifully with either a red or a white wine (there's even a little Chardonnay *in* the sauce). This dish is so packed with flavor you'll want to eat it every night. Ask your butcher to "french" the pork rack for you.

**RACK OF PORK**

8-bone rack of pork, about 8 lb, frenched

Kosher salt and freshly ground black pepper

2 Tbsp grapeseed oil

**MUSTARD SAUCE**

2 Tbsp grapeseed oil

4 cups thinly sliced yellow onions

1 Tbsp unsalted butter

½ cup **James Gang Reserve** Chardonnay

1 cup heavy cream

2 Tbsp Dijon mustard

3 Tbsp pickled mustard seeds or whole-grain mustard

Kosher salt and freshly ground black pepper

### roast the rack of pork

Preheat the oven to 350°F. Bring the pork rack to room temperature, 15 to 20 minutes. Season the rack on all sides with a generous amount of salt and pepper.

In a large cast-iron frying pan over high heat, warm the oil until it begins to smoke lightly. Add the pork rack and brown it on all sides. It takes about 1 minute on each side to get a golden brown crust. Creating a crust on the outside of the pork is a *must* to lock in some serious flavor. Don't forget both ends!

Transfer the pan to the oven and roast the pork until an instant-read thermometer inserted into the thickest part of the meat away from bone registers 148°F, about 45 minutes.

While the pork is roasting, fire up your grill for direct grilling over high heat and make the sauce.

### make the mustard sauce

In a large sauté pan over medium-high heat, warm the oil until it begins to smoke lightly. Add the onions and cook, stirring constantly, until they start to brown, about 10 minutes, then turn down the heat to medium. Add the butter and cook, stirring every 2 minutes, until the onions are golden brown all the way through and very soft, about 10 minutes.

Add the wine, turn down the heat to low, and simmer until the wine has almost totally evaporated, about 2 minutes. Then add the cream, mustard, and mustard seeds, bring to a quick simmer, and stir the sauce to mix well. Season with salt and pepper to taste. Remove from the heat and cover to keep warm.

Remove the pork from the oven and let rest for 15 minutes. The finished internal temperature should register over 150°F.

---

**CHEF PRO TIP:** The reason you let meat "rest" when you take it out of the oven is because it will continue to "cook" for a little while. It's called "carryover cooking."

---

After the pork has rested, slice the pork between every other bone (each double chop should have two bones) to yield four double chops.

### grill the pork chops

Place the pork chops on the cooking grate directly over the fire and grill lightly, turning once, to add some color and flavor, about 1 minute on each side. This step is optional because the pork is already cooked, but a quick trip to the grill makes the chop look great and taste even better.

Serve the pork chops with a generous helping of the sauce and a "double" pour of your favorite Tobin James wine.

WINE PAIRING

*James Gang Reserve* **Chardonnay**

*Midnight Magic* **Petite Sirah**

*Silver Reserve* **Petite Sirah**

*Silver Reserve* **Zinfandel**

**PREP TIME**
15 TO 20 MINUTES

**COOK TIME**
1 HOUR

**MAKES**
4 SERVINGS

**GF**

# rack of lamb with mint *pistou*

The rich, gamy flavor of a rack of lamb demands an equally robust pairing—both on the plate and in your glass. That's why it goes so well with a rough-and-ready mint *pistou* and a nice **Silver Reserve** Petite Sirah or **Chateau Le Cacheflo**. *Pistou* is a rough-chopped basil pesto originally from Provence. Our version is jam-packed with herbaceous flavors, lively citrus notes, and a nice briny tang (from the capers). It's got a lot going on. If you're looking to impress your guests, this divine dish will not disappoint. Ask your butcher to "french" the lamb racks for you.

## WINE PAIRING

*5* Bordeaux Style Blend

*Silver Reserve* Petite Sirah

*Chateau Le Cacheflo*

## MINT *PISTOU*

1½ Tbsp chopped fresh mint leaves

¼ cup finely diced celery

2 Tbsp chopped pine nuts

2 Tbsp chopped capers

1 Tbsp finely diced shallot

1 Tbsp chopped fresh flat-leaf parsley leaves

Finely grated zest of 1 lemon

Finely grated zest of 1 lime

Finely grated zest of 1 orange

1 Tbsp thinly sliced green onion, white and green parts

¼ tsp red pepper flakes

1½ to 2 cups extra-virgin olive oil

Kosher salt and freshly ground black pepper

## LAMB RACKS

2 racks of lamb, about 2 lb (8 bones) each, frenched

Kosher salt and freshly ground black pepper

2 Tbsp grapeseed oil

½ cup Dijon mustard

### make the mint *pistou*

In a medium glass or stainless-steel bowl, combine the mint, celery, pine nuts, capers, shallot, parsley, lemon zest, lime zest, orange zest, green onion, and pepper flakes. Add enough of the olive oil just to cover all the ingredients and stir to combine. Now taste the *pistou* and season with salt and pepper. Cover and refrigerate while you cook the lamb.

### roast the lamb

Preheat the oven to 450°F. Bring the lamb racks to room temperature, about 10 minutes. Season generously on all sides with salt and pepper.

In a large cast-iron frying pan over high heat, warm the grapeseed oil until it begins to smoke lightly. Add the lamb racks and brown them on all sides. It takes 3 to 5 minutes on each side to get a golden brown crust. While the lamb is browning, set a roasting rack on a sheet pan, then transfer the lamb to the rack when it is ready. If you don't have a roasting rack, remove all the oil from the frying pan and roast the lamb in the pan.

Rub the mustard on the lamb, coating the meat completely. Roast until an instant-read thermometer inserted into the thickest part of the rack away from bone registers 130°F, 12 to 15 minutes. Remove from the oven and let rest for 10 minutes. While the lamb is resting, take the *pistou* out of the fridge to bring it back to room temperature.

**CHEF PRO TIP:** It's important to let the lamb "rest" for a while after you take it out of the oven. If you carve it right away, you'll lose the meat juices and dry out the lamb you've worked so hard on!

Slice each lamb rack between every other bone. Each rack will yield four two-bone chops. Serve the chops with the *pistou* and a luscious glass of our **5 Bordeaux Style Blend**!

**PREP TIME**
20 TO 25 MINUTES (PLUS 30 MINUTES TO CHILL)

**COOK TIME**
30 MINUTES

**MAKES**
4 SERVINGS

GF

# rock-n-roll syrah braised lamb shank

Some recipes call for a hint of wine. Not this one. You're going to need a *whole bottle* of *Rock-N-Roll* Syrah to make this dish! And not just for drinking while you wait for the lamb to braise. Braising is all about slow cooking the meat to give it time to soak up all that delicious wine and the distinctive, earthy flavors of other ingredients until the meat melts off the bone. Decadent. Rich. Bold. This meat lover's dish puts the wine where it belongs—at the heart of the meal. You're definitely going to taste the wine in every bite of this dish. That's why we suggest using a high-quality red like our *Rock-N-Roll* Syrah. "Braise the roof" with this slow-cooked crowd-pleaser, and make sure you have another bottle of wine ready for your glasses!

**ROSEMARY OIL**

3 Tbsp chopped fresh rosemary leaves

1 Tbsp chopped garlic

2 Tbsp extra-virgin olive oil

**LAMB SHANKS**

2 Tbsp grapeseed oil

Kosher salt and freshly ground black pepper

4 lamb shanks, about 5 lb total weight

2 cups chopped yellow onions

1 cup sliced peeled carrots, in ¼-inch-thick rounds

1 cup chopped celery

10 garlic cloves, minced

One 750-ml bottle *Rock-N-Roll* Syrah

One 28-oz can diced tomatoes with juices

1¾ cups chicken stock, homemade (page 206) or purchased

1¾ cups beef stock, homemade (page 207) or purchased

5 tsp fresh rosemary leaves, chopped

2 tsp fresh thyme leaves, chopped

2 tsp finely grated lemon zest

## make the rosemary oil

In a small bowl, stir together the rosemary, garlic, and olive oil. Let sit until you're ready to serve. That's it. Cooking is easy, right?

**CHEF PRO TIP:** You can actually make this dish the day before serving and refrigerate it. The lamb shanks will pick up more flavor the longer they steep in the braising liquid. Braised dishes almost always taste better if you let them sit overnight to allow the flavors to blend, but it's not essential.

## braise the lamb shanks

In a large, heavy pot over medium-high heat, warm the oil until it begins to smoke lightly. Meanwhile, sprinkle shanks on all sides with salt and pepper. When the oil is ready, add two shanks to the pot and cook, turning as needed, until a nice brown crust forms on all sides, about 8 minutes total. Transfer the shanks to a large bowl. Brown the remaining two shanks the same way and add them to the bowl.

Add the onions, carrots, celery, and garlic to the pot and cook, stirring occasionally, until golden, about 10 minutes. Add wine, tomatoes and their juices, chicken stock, beef stock, rosemary, thyme, and lemon zest and stir well. Return all the shanks to the pot, pressing down on them to submerge them in the liquid, and bring the liquid to a boil. As soon as the liquid starts to bubble, turn down the heat to low, cover, and simmer gently until the meat is tender but not yet pulling away from the bones. This usually takes about 2 hours, but you'll want to check on it halfway through.

## make the wine reduction

When the meat is tender, uncover the pot and continue to simmer over low heat for 30 minutes. You're trying to let some of the liquid evaporate to reduce the sauce. Once the meat is tender enough to pull away from the bone, transfer the lamb shanks to a platter and tent with aluminum foil (the foil helps to keep them warm). Turn up the heat to medium-high and boil the liquid in the pot until it starts to thicken, about 15 minutes.

Remove from heat and season with salt and pepper. Spoon this glorious red wine reduction and the rosemary oil over the shanks and serve.

If you decide to refrigerate the lamb shanks overnight, reheat them in their sauce over medium heat the next day, then transfer to a platter, spoon the sauce over the top, and finish with the rosemary oil.

BRAISE THE ROOF!

## WINE PAIRING

*Rock-N-Roll* Syrah

*GSM* Blend

**PREP TIME**
25 TO 30 MINUTES

**COOK TIME**
3 TO 3½ HOURS

**MAKES**
4 SERVINGS

**GF**

Claire and Lance Silver enjoy a barrel sampling.

# the big deal bolognese pasta

There's nothing quite like the taste of homemade pasta, especially if you cut the noodles and make the sauce yourself! The beauty of this traditional Bolognese recipe is that you can use your favorite meat (lamb, beef, chicken, or veal) or mix of meats to tailor every bite. Cut the pasta sheets into broad pappardelle or ribbons of tagliatelle for a custom-made Italian feast. And don't forget to bring your appetite! This recipe makes four to six mouthwatering servings of the best Bolognese you'll have this side of Italy.

**WINE PAIRING**

*Dusi Vineyard* **Zinfandel**

*James Gang Reserve* **Zinfandel**

**or any of your favorite Zins**

**PREP TIME**
15 TO 20 MINUTES
(PLUS 1 HOUR IF MAKING FRESH PASTA)

**COOK TIME**
45 TO 60 MINUTES

**MAKES**
4 TO 6 SERVINGS

2 Tbsp grapeseed oil

1½ cups finely diced yellow onions

1 cup finely diced celery

¾ cup finely diced peeled carrot

1 lb grass-fed ground beef (90/10)

4 garlic cloves, minced (about 1 Tbsp)

3 Tbsp tomato paste

1 cup *Primo* **Sangiovese**

2 cups beef stock, homemade (page 207) or purchased

1 cup whole milk

2 bay leaves

¼ tsp ground cinnamon

⅛ tsp freshly grated nutmeg

Kosher salt and freshly ground black pepper

Six to eight 12- by 14-inch long fresh pasta sheets (page 110) or 1 lb purchased fresh fettuccine

Extra-virgin olive oil for drizzling

Grated Parmesan cheese for serving

Fresh oregano or basil leaves for garnish

### make the sauce

In a Dutch oven or other large, heavy pot over high heat, warm the oil until it starts to smoke lightly. Add the onions, celery, and carrots and cook, stirring occasionally, until golden brown, about 5 minutes. Add the beef and continue to cook, breaking up the meat and stirring often, until cooked through, 5 to 8 minutes. Make sure the beef is broken up into small pieces with no large chunks. Add the garlic and tomato paste and cook, stirring, just long enough to cook out the raw tomato flavor, about 1 minute.

**CHEF PRO TIP:** You can use any kind of ground meat (or even vegan substitutes) for this Bolognese. But whatever you use, leaner is always better. Also, when finely dicing the onions, celery, and carrot, try to cut them the same size as cooked ground beef.

Pour in the wine and deglaze the pot, stirring to scrape up the browned bits from the bottom with a wooden spoon. Turn down the heat to medium and simmer until the wine is reduced by half, about 10 minutes.

Add the stock, milk, bay leaves, cinnamon, and nutmeg and stir well. Turn down the heat to medium-low and simmer, stirring occasionally, for 30 minutes. The sauce should

be lightly bubbling. You can cover the pot to keep the sauce from splattering, but leave it cracked so steam can escape. You want the sauce to reduce down to a chili-like consistency (about 4 to 6 cups). Once the sauce is reduced to your desired thickness, remove the bay leaves and season with salt and pepper.

### cook the pasta

In a large pot over high heat, bring 5 qt water to a rolling boil. Once it starts boiling, add 1 Tbsp salt. If you're using fresh pasta sheets, cut the noodles while you're waiting for the water to boil.

Grab a knife and cut each sheet lengthwise into five or six slices. If you prefer wider noodles, cut fewer slices. The beauty of fresh pasta is that the size of the noodles is up to you.

Once the noodles are cut, add them to the salted boiling water and stir gently to keep them from sticking together. Cook the pasta for 2 to 3 minutes. It should be tender and cooked through but not soft.

Drain the noodles, divide them among individual plates, and drizzle each portion with a little olive oil. Top each serving with a nice scoop of the Bolognese sauce and then garnish with Parmesan and oregano. Serve at once. There's nothing like sitting down to homemade Italian food and a great bottle of red. *Bellissimo!*

# grilled ny strip with smoked onion butter

**WINE PAIRING**

*Private Stash*

*James Gang Reserve* Syrah

*Schist* Portuguese Blend

*Palindrome* Tannat

A New York strip steak tends to be a little less tender than a fillet, but it's packed with rich, beefy flavor. All you need to do to serve a great strip steak is to sear it and add butter. We love the complex smoky and sweet notes of this butter because they really elevate the dish, making it a great wine-friendly entrée. As long as you have a bottle of Tobin James handy, you can't go wrong with this incredible steak. Just make sure you have enough *Private Stash* for seconds!

## CHIMICHURRI STEAK MARINADE

½ Tbsp minced garlic

½ Tbsp chopped fresh oregano

2 Tbsp extra-virgin olive oil

1 tsp red wine vinegar

1 tsp freshly ground black pepper

Pinch of kosher salt

4 New York strip steaks, each about 6 oz

## SMOKED ONION BUTTER

½ cup diced yellow onion

½ cup unsalted butter, at room temperature

1 tsp chopped fresh flat-leaf parsley leaves

Kosher salt and freshly ground black pepper

1 Tbsp grapeseed oil

4 green onions, root ends trimmed

### marinate the steaks

In a small glass or stainless-steel bowl, stir together the garlic, oregano, olive oil, vinegar, pepper, and salt. Put the steaks into a baking dish or pan, pour the marinade over the top, and turn to coat evenly. Cover and marinate in the refrigerator for at least 1 hour or up to 2 hours.

### make the smoked onion butter

Preheat your smoker to 350°F on high smoke. Smoke the yellow onion until brown and soft, 45 minutes to 1 hour. Remove from the smoker and let cool.

---

**CHEF PRO TIP:** If you don't have a smoker, you can caramelize the onion with a little grapeseed oil in a cast-iron frying pan over medium-high heat on the stove top. When the onion is golden brown, remove from the heat and mix in ¼ tsp liquid smoke.

---

In a small bowl, combine the smoked onion, butter, and parsley and season with salt and pepper. Stir until well mixed, then set aside.

### cook the steaks

Preheat the oven to 350°F. In a large cast-iron pan over high heat, warm the grapeseed oil until it smokes lightly. Add the steaks and sear, turning once, until both sides have a nice crispy crust, about 3 minutes on each side.

Transfer the pan to the oven and cook the steaks to your desired doneness. We recommend 130°F for medium rare, which will take 3 to 5 minutes.

Transfer the steaks to a large plate and top each one with a generous scoop of the smoked onion butter. Let the steaks rest for 5 minutes. Pour yourself a glass of *Private Stash* or *James Gang Reserve* Syrah and watch the butter melt into a gooey dream.

Empty out any juice from the cast-iron pan and place it over medium-high heat. Add the green onions and sear, turning as needed, until they begin to soften and char. Less is more.

Slice the steaks and plate them with the charred green onions. You can even pour the excess melted butter back on top of the steaks. Serve at once.

**PREP TIME**
30 MINUTES
(PLUS AT LEAST 1 HOUR TO MARINATE)

**COOK TIME**
1 HOUR

**MAKES**
4 SERVINGS

GF

# coffee-rubbed filet mignon

Why would you ever want to rub ground coffee all over your beautiful filet mignon? Because the earthiness and texture of the coffee (and other spices!) complement the cracked black pepper, giving the meat a wonderful spicy finish. Serve with oven-roasted onion cups and a complex and beautiful red wine demi-glace that slices through the richness of the meat with balanced acidity. If you don't want to make the demi-glace, we like the More Than Gourmet brand. Pair this meal with your best red wine, like our *5 Bordeaux Style Blend* or *Blue Moon Reserve* Cabernet Sauvignon, for a decadent dish that will make your mouth water.

## WINE PAIRING

*5* Bordeaux Style Blend

*James Gang Reserve* Cabernet Sauvignon

*Blue Moon Reserve* Cabernet Sauvignon

**PREP TIME**
30 TO 40 MINUTES

**COOK TIME**
45 MINUTES

**MAKES**
4 SERVINGS

GF

## RED WINE DEMI-GLACE

1 cup *James Gang Reserve* Cabernet Sauvignon

1 cup veal demi-glace, homemade (page 208) or purchased

## ONION CUPS

1 large yellow onion

1 Tbsp grapeseed oil

## COFFEE RUB

2 Tbsp finely ground coffee

1 Tbsp kosher or flaked salt

1 Tbsp freshly ground black pepper

1 tsp dark brown sugar

Four 5 oz filet mignons

2 Tbsp grapeseed oil

2 cups Salt-Roasted Beets, cut into ¼-inch cubes (page 203)

Cauliflower Purée, warmed (page 201)

¼ cup loosely packed fresh sage leaves for garnish (optional)

### make the red wine demi-glace

In a small saucepan over medium heat, bring the wine to a simmer and simmer until reduced to ¼ cup, 8 to 10 minutes. Add the veal demi-glace and continue to simmer until the mixture is reduced to about 1 cup, 8 to 10 minutes. Keep warm until serving.

### make the onion cups

Preheat the oven to 450°F. Heat a small cast-iron frying pan on the stove top over medium heat. While the pan is heating, cut the onion in half through the stem end and peel off the skin from each half. Add the grapeseed oil to the hot pan, and when the oil begins to smoke lightly, add the onion halves, cut side down, and sear until golden brown, about 2 minutes. Transfer the pan to the oven and roast the onion halves until the onion is cooked through and softened, about 20 minutes.

Remove the pan from the oven. Leave the oven on at 350°F (you'll need it for the steaks). Gently remove the onion halves from the pan. The cut sides should be charred and very dark. Once the onion halves cool, separate them into onion "petal" cups. These cups will hold the demi-glace (see photo).

### make the coffee rub

In a small bowl, stir together the coffee, salt, pepper, and brown sugar.

### cook the steaks

Heat a large cast-iron frying pan over medium-high heat. While the pan is heating, generously coat the steaks on all sides with the coffee rub. Add the grapeseed oil to the hot pan, and when the oil begins to smoke lightly, add the steaks and sear, turning once, until both sides have a nice crispy crust, about 2 minutes.

Transfer the pan to the oven and cook the steaks to your desired doneness. We recommend 130°F for medium rare, which will take 2 to 3 minutes.

To serve, transfer the steaks to a large plate and tent with aluminum foil to keep warm. Add the beets to the cast-iron pan to warm them from the residual heat. Ladle some demi-glace into the onion cups.

Slice the steaks and plate them. Serve with the beets, the onion cups, and a smear of cauliflower purée and the optional sage for a delicious, elegant, wine-friendly meal.

**CHEF PRO TIP:** For a touch of extra crunch, deep-fry the sage leaves in grapeseed oil heated to 350°F for 1 minute.

# "slow jams" zinfandel jam burger

## WINE PAIRING

*Ballistic* **Zinfandel**

*Fat Boy* **Zinfandel**

*the blend*

Finally, a burger custom-built for wine lovers! Dressed up with a wine-based bacon-infused "marmalade," heirloom tomatoes, grilled onions, crisp dill pickles, and a creamy Thousand Island–style spread, this next-level burger not only tastes delicious but also pairs *perfectly* with red wine! If you're someone who craves a good burger (like Lance!), you can match this tower of beefy goodness with a glass of *Ballistic* or *Fat Boy* **Zinfandel** or *the blend* and take your burger addiction to new heights.

## THOUSAND ISLAND DRESSING

¼ cup mayonnaise

2 Tbsp chopped capers

2 Tbsp finely diced shallot

1 Tbsp pickled mustard seeds or whole-grain mustard

1 tsp smoked paprika

1 tsp ketchup

1 tsp fresh lemon juice

## BURGERS

4 grass-fed beef burger patties, each about 8 oz

Kosher salt and freshly ground black pepper

2 tsp yellow mustard

2 Tbsp grapeseed oil

4 slices sharp Cheddar cheese

4 sesame seed buns, split

4 Bibb lettuce leaves

4 thin slices red onion

4 slices heirloom tomato (optional)

1 avocado, halved, pitted, peeled, and sliced

½ cup Bacon-Onion Marmalade (page 209)

4 dill pickle spears

## make the thousand island dressing

In a small bowl, combine the mayonnaise, capers, shallot, mustard seeds, paprika, ketchup, and lemon juice and mix well. It's literally that easy.

## cook the burgers

Season the burger patties on both sides with salt and pepper, then lightly brush both sides with the yellow mustard. Heat a large cast-iron frying pan over medium-high heat. When the pan is hot, add 1 Tbsp of the oil and heat until it begins to smoke lightly. Add two burger patties and sear for 2 minutes on each side until a crust forms. Once you flip the burgers, add a slice of cheese to each one so the cheese gets nice and melty. Transfer the burgers to a plate and repeat with the remaining oil, patties, and cheese.

---

**CHEF PRO TIP:** A cook time of 4 minutes is good for medium rare. You can cook a burger longer if that's how you like it.

---

Now toast the buns, cut side down, in the same pan. When they are done, it's time to build the burger.

## build the burger

Here's how we make it:

Spread the bun bottom with 1 Tbsp Thousand Island dressing, then top with:

1 lettuce leaf
1 onion slice
1 tomato slice
A few avocado slices
Burger patty with cheese
A generous spoonful of the "marmalade"
The bun top

Hi-five!

Serve with a dill pickle spear and your favorite potato chips. It's the perfect burger for your favorite **Tobin James Zin**!

**PREP TIME**
25 MINUTES

**COOK TIME**
10 MINUTES (PLUS 30 MINUTES FOR THE "MARMALADE")

**MAKES**
4 SERVINGS

DREAMS DO COME TRUE...

COME CRUISE
WITH US!

# cruisin' braised beef short ribs

Honed over the years, this short rib recipe is an all-time favorite from our Tobin James cruises! And the best part about these beef ribs is that you can customize the sauce to your palate. Add a touch of sweetness with brown sugar or honey, or keep it wine focused and more savory. No matter how you like your ribs, you're sure to be satisfied, especially if you open a bottle of our *5 Bordeaux Style Blend*. Make a batch of oven-roasted seasonal vegetables to accompany the ribs and potatoes.

4 boneless beef short ribs, each about 6 oz

Kosher salt and freshly ground black pepper

2 Tbsp grapeseed oil

1 cup diced yellow onion

1 cup diced peeled carrots

1 cup diced celery

8 garlic cloves, minced

One 750-ml bottle **5 Bordeaux Style Blend**

One 28 oz can crushed tomatoes with juices

3 cups beef or veal stock, homemade (page 207) or purchased

12 fresh thyme sprigs

3 bay leaves (dried or fresh)

3 fresh basil leaves

¼ cup honey or loosely packed dark brown sugar (optional)

Rosemary Poppin' Potatoes (page 200)

Season the beef ribs on all sides with salt and pepper. In a large cast-iron frying pan over medium-high heat, warm 2 Tbsp of the oil until it begins to smoke lightly. Add the ribs and sear on all sides until a crust forms, about 2 minutes on each side. Transfer the ribs to a plate.

Add the onion, carrots, and celery to the pan and sauté until slightly soft, about 5 minutes. Add the garlic and cook until it softens, about 1 minute. Pour in the wine and deglaze the pan, stirring to scrape up the browned bits from the bottom with a wooden spoon. Lower the heat to medium and simmer until the alcohol is cooked off, 3 to 5 minutes.

Return the ribs to the pan and add the tomatoes, stock, thyme, bay leaves, basil, and enough water to cover the ribs (about 1 cup). Bring to a gentle simmer, cover, and simmer until the ribs are fork-tender and almost falling apart. This can take up to 1 hour. If the liquid gets too thick, add a little water.

**CHEF PRO TIP:** The term *fork-tender* means you can push a meat fork through the center of a piece of meat without much resistance. The longer you cook the ribs, the more tender they get, and the better they taste!

When the ribs are done, transfer them to a plate and keep warm. With the pan uncovered, simmer the sauce over medium heat until it is thick enough to coat the back of a spoon, 10 to 15 minutes.

Remove the sauce from the heat and pour it through a fine-mesh sieve to remove the solids. You want a smooth, fairly thick sauce. Return the sauce to the pan. If the sauce is too runny, place the pan over medium-low heat and simmer until the sauce has reduced and thickened. If you like your ribs sweet, stir in the honey or brown sugar.

Return the ribs to the sauce and reheat over medium heat until hot, about 2 minutes. Season with a pinch each of salt and pepper. Serve the ribs with the potatoes and open a bottle of any of our Cabs or Bordeaux style blends.

## WINE PAIRING

*Notorious* **Cabernet Sauvignon**

**5 Bordeaux Style Blend**

*Blue Moon Reserve* **Cabernet Sauvignon**

*Schist* **Portuguese Blend**

**PREP TIME**
20 TO 25 MINUTES

**COOK TIME**
1½ TO 2 HOURS

**MAKES**
4 SERVINGS

GF

## MEAT SAUCE

½ cup grapeseed oil

4 lb grass-fed ground beef (90/10)

1 cup olive oil

2 cups chopped yellow onions

1 carrot, peeled and grated

8 to 10 garlic cloves, minced

¼ cup tomato paste

4 cups beef stock, homemade (page 207) or purchased

2 tsp red pepper flakes (optional)

2 cups whole milk

4 egg yolks

Kosher salt and freshly ground black pepper

## LASAGNA

One 9 oz box "no boil" lasagna noodles

12 cups shredded mozzarella cheese (3 lb)

1 bunch fresh flat-leaf parsley, chopped

1 cup grated Parmesan cheese

Fresh basil leaves for garnish

1½ cups Chef Marc's Marinara Sauce (page 210), Besciamella with Parmesan Cheese Sauce (page 210), or your favorite purchased marinara sauce (optional; see **CHEF PRO TIP**)

# "not your average" lasagna

So you're having a bunch of people over for dinner. No problem. We think this delicious twist on an Italian classic is the perfect dish for entertaining large groups—especially if you're going to open a few too many bottles of wine! Pair this simple yet elevated classic with just about any decadent Italian-style red for a special occasion or a boisterous night with close friends. Either way, this isn't your average lasagna. If you have leftovers, this is a great dish to cut into squares and save in the freezer. It also makes a delicious, satisfying meal the next day without any mess. Talk about perfection! *Chef's kiss*

## WINE PAIRING

*Fat Boy* Zinfandel

*Pasorolo* Nebbiolo

**PREP TIME**
45 MINUTES

**COOK TIME**
45 MINUTES

**MAKES**
6 TO 8 SERVINGS (YOU MIGHT HAVE LEFTOVERS!)

### make the meat sauce

Preheat the oven to 350°F. Coat the bottom of a deep cast-iron or enameled pot (like a Le Creuset) with the grapeseed oil. Add the ground beef, spreading it out on the bottom of the pot, and then turn on the heat to high. Cook until the beef is browned on the underside, about 5 minutes. Continue to cook, breaking up the beef and stirring, until all the beef is brown—not gray—and the fat starts to simmer and boil, 5 to 8 minutes. Turn down the heat to low and let simmer.

While the beef is browning, in a medium saucepan over medium heat, warm the olive oil. Add the onions, carrot, and garlic and cook, stirring occasionally, until golden brown and delicious, 10 to 15 minutes. Add the tomato paste and cook, stirring, for another 5 minutes to bring out the flavors.

Pour the vegetable mixture into the beef pot and stir to combine. Add the stock and pepper flakes (if using), raise the heat to medium, bring to a boil, and boil gently to reduce and let everything come together. This should take about 15 minutes. Stir every 3 to 5 minutes so nothing burns.

Once the mixture has reduced down to a thick sauce, stir in 1 cup of the milk. Reduce the sauce again, another 5 minutes, then add the remaining 1 cup milk and reduce once more. Remove the pot from the heat and stir in the egg yolks. The egg yolks will cook in the residual heat, so keep stirring until they emulsify with the meat sauce. Season the sauce with salt and pepper.

Now it's time to assemble the lasagna!

### assemble the lasagna

Ladle about 1 cup of the meat sauce onto the bottom of an 11- by 16-inch baking dish and cover with a layer of the noodles. Top with a thicker layer of meat sauce (2 to 3 cups), followed by a layer of mozzarella (about 3 cups), and then another layer of noodles. Add the parsley to the next layer. Add another layer of meat sauce (2 to 3 cups) and a layer of mozzarella (about 3 cups). Add a last noodle layer, a meat sauce layer (2 to 3 cups), a mozzarella layer (about 3 cups), and finish with a layer of Parmesan, spreading evenly over the top. Congratulations, you've just built a really tall and complicated lasagna tower.

Bake the lasagna until the top is golden brown, 30 to 35 minutes. Then enjoy a glass of **Fat Boy** Zin while you let the lasagna rest for about 10 minutes or so. Garnish with the basil, then serve.

**CHEF PRO TIP:** This lasagna stands alone. But if you like your lasagna with a little extra, top individual portions with Chef Marc's Marinara Sauce, our creamy Besciamella with Parmesan Cheese Sauce, or your favorite marinara sauce. We like it with *both* marinara and Besciamella sauce! Yum!

pizza

If you've ever been to one of our parties or events at the winery, you know about our handcrafted pizzas. Chef Marc has been slinging his unique repertoire of signature gourmet pies for over ten years, and one thing has remained the same over the past decade: if you snooze you lose! Luckily, we've compiled Chef Marc's most popular pizza recipes here—including how he makes that delicious dough from scratch!—so you can feed the hungry masses at your house. But be warned, you're probably going to have to make more than one pizza to keep everyone happy!

# pizza dough

Spoiler alert: Making pizza dough from scratch is pretty technical—almost like baking. But if you follow these directions, you can make a great homemade pizza crust with a stand mixer or, if you're old-school, by hand. This recipe is for two dough balls (enough for two small pizzas). But you're welcome to double the recipe for four pizzas, triple it for six, and so on. Making your own dough is tough, but it's worth the effort. However, if you don't have the time or the energy, you can always use store-bought dough for any of the pizza recipes in this chapter. As long as you have a bottle of Tobin James, everything will be fine. This recipe works best with a stand mixer. You can make the dough completely by hand, but it's definitely more work. Steps for handmade dough follow the stand mixer directions.

225 g lukewarm water

5 g instant yeast

350 g 'OO' pizza flour or all-purpose flour

6 g kosher salt

## make pizza dough in a stand mixer

1. In the bowl of a stand mixer, stir together the water and yeast.

2. Let the mixture sit for 1 minute, or until the yeast dissolves.

3. Add the flour and salt to the yeast mixture. Fit the mixer with the dough hook and beat on low speed for 10 minutes, scraping down the sides of the bowl now and again to make sure nothing is sticking. Mixing the dough this long will develop the gluten.

CHEF PRO TIP: You want a smooth, white dough with no lumps. It should be tacky to the touch but barely stick to your fingers (not too dry or too sticky). If the dough feels too dry, add a couple of drops of water and remix until the water is absorbed. If the dough is too wet, add a few tsp of flour and remix.

4. Lightly coat a glass or stainless-steel bowl with cooking spray.

5. Use a dough scraper or spatula to transfer the dough to the prepared bowl. Cover the bowl with plastic wrap.

6. Let the dough rise until it roughly doubles in size, about 1 hour.

## THE DOUGH WHISPERER

**make pizza dough by hand**

If you don't have a stand mixer, you can make the dough by hand in a large bowl. It will just be a little messier—and use a lot more elbow grease!

In a large glass or stainless-steel bowl, stir together the water and yeast.

Let the mixture sit for 1 minute, or until the yeast is dissolved.

Add the flour and salt and mix with your hands until you get a smooth, white dough ball. You should get a dough ball within 5 minutes of mixing. Once that ball forms, turn the dough out onto a lightly floured work surface. You still need to knead (ha!) the dough for another 5 minutes. If the dough is too sticky, dust your hands with flour or rub with a little oil.

Now follow steps 4 through 10 in Make Pizza Dough in a Stand Mixer.

**PREP TIME**
15 MINUTES (PLUS
2 HOURS TO RISE)

**MAKES**
TWO 10 OZ DOUGH BALLS

7. Remove the plastic wrap. Lightly dust your hands with flour. With the dough still in the bowl, push down on the dough to push out all the excess air. This is called "punching down the dough."

8. Spray a sheet pan with cooking spray. Divide the dough in half and shape each half into a ball (each about 10 oz). Place the balls on the prepared sheet pan.

9. Lightly coat the top of each dough ball with cooking spray. Lightly cover the sheet pan with plastic wrap (to keep the dough moist) and let the dough balls rise until they roughly double in size, about 1 hour.

10. After the dough has risen a second time, it is ready to shape into a pizza crust. Turn the page for instructions on stretching the dough. You can also store the dough, tightly covered, in the fridge for up to 24 hours. Use the freezer for anything longer (up to 6 months).

# stretching the dough & baking the pizza

Making a pizza from scratch is a rite of passage. It's difficult, but mastering the art of pizza at home is a great way to craft your own perfect pie. Every kitchen is a little different, so feel free to tweak these directions as you go. Make sure you have one or two bottles of wine handy to toast your success—and to get you through any rough spots! Here's how to make a spectacular pizza at home just like the pros.

Pizza Dough (page 178)

Semolina flour or cornmeal for dusting

All-purpose flour for dusting

**Preheat the oven.** Position a rack in the lower third of the oven, place a pizza stone on the rack, and preheat the oven to 550°F (or higher if possible) for at least 30 minutes before baking. If you don't have a pizza stone, you can use an over-turned sheet pan, but don't preheat it in the oven. Just slip it onto the oven rack about 5 minutes before you are ready to slide the pizza onto it.

**Prep the dough.** If you refrigerated the dough balls, let them come to room temperature for at least 30 minutes while the oven is heating.

**Dust the pizza peel.** Generously dust a pizza peel, an over-turned sheet pan, or a rimless cookie sheet with semolina flour. The flour will prevent the dough from sticking to the wood or metal. It's what makes the pizza "slide" off the peel.

**Transfer the dough.** Make the pizzas one at a time. Lightly flour a hard work surface, like a countertop or cutting board, with all-purpose flour. Dip your hands—including the backs of your hands and knuckles—into all-purpose flour and lift one dough ball by getting under it with a pastry scraper or thin metal spatula. Place the dough ball on the floured surface (photo 1).

**Stretch the dough.** With your fingertips, press the dough flat, keeping it in a circle (photo 2). Then pull the dough from opposite sides to stretch it (photo 3), moving all the way around the dough. You should end up with a round, flat piece of dough about 8 inches in diameter (photo 4).

**Bounce the dough.** Make your hands into fists, gently lay the dough across your knuckles, and carefully stretch it by bouncing it in a circular motion on your hands, giving it a little stretch

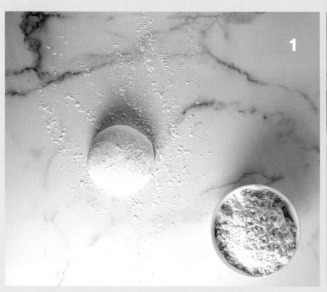

with each bounce (photo 5). This is the fun part! If it starts to stick to your hands, lay the dough down on the floured countertop and dust your hands with a little more flour. Then continue bouncing the dough until it is 10 to 12 inches in diameter.

If you're having trouble getting the "fist-bounce technique" to work, move to a full toss (just like the movies)! We're only half joking about this. The goal is to spread the dough evenly into a thin circle. If the dough keeps springing back, let it rest for another 5 to 20 minutes so the gluten can relax. Then try again. You can also resort to using a rolling pin, though this isn't as effective as the hand-toss method.

**Transfer the pizza.** When the dough is stretched out to your satisfaction (photo 6), lay it on the prepared pizza peel or sheet pan, making sure there is enough semolina flour to allow the dough to slide.

**Top the pizza.** Lightly top the pizza dough with your choice of sauce and toppings.

**Bake the pizza.** Slide the finished pizza off the peel onto the pizza stone (or overturned pan) in the oven and bake! At 10 to 12 minutes, you'll start to see a nice golden brown crust. Lift it up and check the bottom of the crust, too. You might need to rotate the pizza 180 degrees to bake it evenly. Remove the pizza from the oven with a pizza peel (or remove the sheet pan with the pizza on it) and transfer it to a cutting board. Wait for 3 to 5 minutes before slicing and serving, to allow the cheese to set slightly.

**CHEF PRO TIP:** Don't load up your pizza crust with too much sauce and dozens of toppings. If you do, the sauce will overflow, the toppings won't cook evenly, and you will make a huge mess. This is homemade dough. It's fragile. Keep it to no more than a small ladle of sauce, three or four toppings, and a sprinkle of cheese and you'll do just fine. Embrace this less-is-more philosophy and you'll have a much better pizza. Save the more-is-more philosophy for your wineglass.

**PREP TIME**
30 MINUTES

**MAKES**
TWO 10- TO 12-INCH PIZZAS

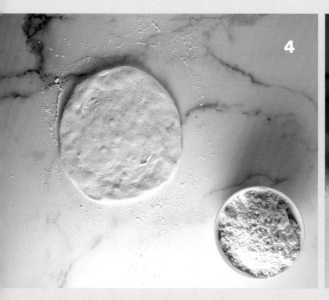

THAT'S AMORE!

# chef marc's world-famous pizza sauce extravaganza

If you've ever had one of our "gone-in-two-seconds" pizzas at a Tobin James event and wondered what the "secret sauce" is, you're in luck. This is literally the recipe for the pizza sauce that we've refined over the years for all our Tobin James pizza parties, BBQs, and winery events. The blend of herbs, garlic, and a touch of sweetness balances the acidity of the tomatoes for a delicious sauce that will enhance just about any pizza you choose to make.

**PREP TIME**
5 TO 10 MINUTES (PLUS
30 MINUTES TO CHILL)

**MAKES**
ABOUT 1¾ CUPS;
ENOUGH FOR THREE
10-INCH PIZZAS

**GF/VEG**

One 14 oz can tomato purée

2 garlic cloves, minced

1 Tbsp extra-virgin olive oil

1 Tbsp dark brown sugar

1 tsp honey, warmed

1 tsp minced peeled carrot

½ tsp dried onion powder

¼ tsp dried basil

¼ tsp dried oregano

¼ tsp dried thyme

¼ tsp dried parsley

¼ tsp kosher salt

Freshly ground black pepper

In a large glass or stainless-steel bowl, whisk together all the ingredients until well blended, 1 to 2 minutes. (Warming up the honey a bit will help to ensure it is evenly distributed.)

Once everything is well mixed, cover and refrigerate for at least 30 minutes before using. You can make this the day before. The sauce will keep in an airtight container in the refrigerator for up to 7 days.

**CHEF PRO TIP:** Tomato can stain plastic containers. Always store tomato sauce in a glass or stainless-steel container to avoid unsightly stains.

# marc's basil pesto sauce

This is Chef Marc's go-to pesto recipe. Mix things up with a pesto pizza that your guests will rave about. You'll need only ½ cup pesto for each pizza. You can use the rest for a pasta dish or another pizza.

**PREP TIME**
5 TO 10 MINUTES

**MAKES**
ABOUT 2 CUPS;
ENOUGH FOR FOUR
10-INCH PIZZAS

**GF/VEG**

2 cups tightly packed fresh basil leaves

½ cup grated Parmesan cheese

½ cup pine nuts, toasted

3 garlic cloves, minced

½ tsp fine sea salt

½ tsp freshly ground black pepper

½ cup extra-virgin olive oil

In a food processor or blender, combine the basil, Parmesan, pine nuts, garlic, salt, and pepper and pulse until the basil is finely chopped, about 1 minute. With the food processor or blender running, slowly drizzle in the oil until it is completely incorporated.

Scrape down the sides of the blender, then pulse again until the mixture is smooth. Use immediately or refrigerate in an airtight container with a layer of plastic wrap hugging the top of the pesto for up to 3 days. You can also freeze this sauce for up to 3 months.

**CHEF PRO TIP:** Don't overprocess this sauce. The speed of the blades can heat up and actually "cook" the basil if you process it for too long, turning it an unappetizing dark green.

# white parmesan sauce

**Parmesan cheese in liquid form. Perfection.**

**PREP TIME**
5 MINUTES

**COOK TIME**
7 TO 10 MINUTES

**MAKES**
1 CUP; ENOUGH FOR TWO
10- TO 12-INCH PIZZAS

**VEG**

1 Tbsp unsalted butter

1 Tbsp all-purpose flour

¾ cup low-fat or whole milk

2 garlic cloves, pressed or finely grated

⅛ tsp kosher salt

⅛ tsp freshly ground black pepper

½ cup shredded Parmesan cheese (preferably with a Microplane)

In a small saucepan over medium heat, melt the butter. Whisk in the flour and continue whisking for 1 to 2 minutes (do not let it brown). Slowly add the milk while whisking constantly, then continue to whisk until smooth, thickened, and bubbly, about 5 minutes. Whisk in the garlic, salt, and pepper, then add the Parmesan and whisk for another 30 seconds. Once the cheese is added, do not allow the sauce to boil or it may curdle.

Remove from the heat and continue whisking until the cheese is melted and the sauce is smooth. Set aside to cool before using. It will keep in an airtight container in the refrigerator for up to 5 days.

**CHEF PRO TIP:** The flavor of this cream sauce comes from the quality of the Parmesan cheese. Good cheese makes great sauce!

# the pizza

Chef Marc's command of the wood-fired pizza oven is always the centerpiece of Tobin James' parties and BBQs. And it's no surprise why.

# pear & gorgonzola pizza

Sharp, salty Gorgonzola pairs incredibly well with the sweet, sturdy flavor of pears. Asian pears hold up in cooking better than other pears we've tried (they're almost apple-like), which makes them absolutely perfect for stacking on a homemade pizza! Simple to make yet packed with a heady balance of rich, salty, and semisweet flavors, this pizza is a go-to favorite for just about any Tobin James event. Add a bottle of decadent *James Gang Reserve* Chardonnay and you've got a pair on a pear!

1 tsp unsalted butter

1 Asian pear, halved, cored, and thinly sliced lengthwise

1 tsp dark brown sugar

One 10 oz ball pizza dough, homemade (page 178) or purchased

Semolina or all-purpose flour for dusting

1 Tbsp extra-virgin olive oil

Kosher salt and freshly ground black pepper

½ cup crumbled Gorgonzola cheese

½ cup shredded mozzarella cheese

**make the pear topping**

In a medium sauté pan over medium heat, melt the butter. When it has melted and is bubbling, add the pear slices and brown sugar and cook, stirring occasionally, until the pears are cooked through and the liquid they released starts to thicken and bubble, about 10 minutes. Remove from the heat and let cool.

**make the pizza**

Following the directions in Stretching the Dough & Baking the Pizza on page 180, prepare and preheat the oven to 550°F or higher, then prep the dough, dust the peel, stretch and bounce the dough until it is 10 to 12 inches in diameter, and transfer it to the peel. If you are using a store-bought crust, no worries! Just put it on the dusted peel.

Brush the entire pizza crust with the oil, stopping within about ½ inch of the edge. Lightly season the crust with salt and pepper, then spread the pear slices evenly over the crust. You can drizzle a little of the cooking liquid from the pears on the pizza, but you don't want to soak the dough. Finally, sprinkle the Gorgonzola and mozzarella cheeses evenly over the top.

**bake the pizza**

Slide the finished pizza off the peel onto the pizza stone (or overturned pan) and bake until the crust is a nice golden brown and the cheeses are melted and bubbling, 10 to 12 minutes. Transfer the pizza to a cutting board. Wait for 3 to 5 minutes before slicing and serving to allow the cheeses to set slightly. Open a bottle of Tobin James and enjoy!

**WINE PAIRING**

*James Gang Reserve* Chardonnay

*French Camp Vineyard* Zinfandel

**PREP TIME**
15 TO 20 MINUTES

**COOK TIME**
18 TO 20 MINUTES

**MAKES**
ONE 10- TO 12-INCH PIZZA

**VEG**

# the big dill pickle pizza

Pickles might seem like a strange pizza topping, but the acidity of the dill pickles helps cut through the creamy, cheesy sauce for a balanced—and frankly—unique pizza. Trust us, your friends will be raving about this pizza for years to come, especially when they taste it with a bottle of Tobin James!

One 10-oz ball pizza dough, homemade (page 178) or purchased

Semolina or all-purpose flour for dusting

½ cup White Parmesan Sauce (page 183)

2 cups shredded mozzarella cheese

8 dill pickle sandwich slices

1 tsp chopped fresh dill

### make the pizza

Following the directions in Stretching the Dough & Baking the Pizza on page 180, prepare and preheat the oven to 550°F or higher, then prep the dough, dust the peel, stretch and bounce the dough until it is 10 to 12 inches in diameter, and transfer it to the peel. If you are using a store-bought crust, no worries! Just put it on the dusted peel.

Spread the entire pizza crust with a thin layer of the sauce, stopping within about ½ inch of the edge.

**CHEF PRO TIP:** If you add too much sauce, the extra sauce will probably run off the pizza. Less is more. No soggy bottoms here!

Sprinkle the cheese evenly over the pizza.

Arrange the pickle slices on top, laying them in a spoke pattern from the edge toward the center and spacing them evenly. Bonus points if you can make the pickle slices look like the Tobin James sun!

Slide the finished pizza off the peel onto the pizza stone (or overturned pan) and bake until the crust is a nice golden brown and the cheese is melted and bubbling, 10 to 12 minutes. Transfer the pizza to a cutting board. Wait for 3 to 5 minutes before slicing and serving to allow the cheese to set slightly. Sprinkle with the dill and wind down with a glass of **Tobin James** *Chateau Le Cacheflo*.

## WINE PAIRING

*Radiance* **Chardonnay**

*Chateau Le Cacheflo*

**PREP TIME**
15 TO 20 MINUTES

**COOK TIME**
10 TO 12 MINUTES

**MAKES**
ONE 10- TO 12-INCH PIZZA

**VEG**

YOUR WINE CLUB TEAM. CHEERS!

# too much garlic & shrimp pizza

The heart of this pizza is the garlic. And the best way to prepare garlic is confit style aka "low and slow." This is easily one of the most popular pizzas at our summer events at the winery. And it's all thanks to the garlic. Seriously, it's worth the extra step to confit the garlic in oil instead of just tossing it on the pizza. You'll taste the difference. Here's how to make, quite possibly, the best garlic and shrimp pizza ever created.

**WINE PAIRING**

*Radiance* **Chardonnay**

*James Gang Reserve* **Riesling**

**PREP TIME**
20 TO 25 MINUTES

**COOK TIME**
25 TO 30 MINUTES

**MAKES**
ONE 10- TO 12-INCH PIZZA

**GARLIC CONFIT**

1 cup grapeseed oil

8 garlic cloves, halved lengthwise

**PIZZA**

6 extra-jumbo shrimp (21/25), peeled and deveined

Kosher salt and freshly ground black pepper

2 Tbsp grapeseed oil

One 10-oz ball pizza dough, homemade (page 178) or purchased

All-purpose flour, for dusting

½ cup pesto, homemade (page 183) or purchased

2 cups shredded mozzarella cheese

½ cup julienned zucchini

## make the garlic confit

In a small saucepan over medium heat, combine the oil and garlic and heat slowly until the garlic starts to bubble. Turn down the heat to low and simmer gently until the garlic is golden brown and delicious, about 5 minutes. Remove from the heat and let the garlic cool in the oil.

**CHEF PRO TIP:** You can do this step ahead of time and store the garlic in the oil in an airtight container in the refrigerator for up to 5 days. Be sure to save the oil to use in your other cooking. Yum!

## cook the shrimp

Cut each shrimp in half lengthwise so you have twelve pieces. Season with salt and pepper. In a large sauté pan over medium-high heat, warm the grapeseed oil until it begins to smoke lightly. Add the shrimp and sauté until cooked through, 2 to 3 minutes. Transfer the shrimp to a bowl, let cool for a couple of minutes, and then cover and refrigerate until you are ready to top the pizza.

## make the pizza

Following the directions in Stretching the Dough & Baking the Pizza on page 180, prepare and preheat the oven to 550°F or higher, then prep the dough, dust the peel, stretch and bounce the dough until it is 10 to 12 inches in diameter, and transfer it to the peel. If you are using a store-bought crust, no worries! Just put it on the dusted peel.

Spread the entire pizza crust with the pesto, stopping within about ½ inch of the edge. Top the pizza evenly with the mozzarella. Arrange the garlic on top of the cheese, making sure every slice will get an equal amount of the delicious sweet garlic. Repeat with the shrimp and zucchini, distributing them evenly over the crust.

## bake the pizza

Slide the finished pizza off the peel onto the pizza stone (or overturned pan) and bake until the crust is golden brown and the cheese is melted and bubbling, 10 to 12 minutes, enjoying those yummy garlic aromas while you sip your favorite Tobin James wine. Transfer the pizza to a cutting board. Wait for 3 to 5 minutes before slicing and serving to allow the cheese to set slightly.

# chef's favorite sausage & mushroom pizza with peperoncini

**WINE PAIRING**

*Ballistic*
**Zinfandel**

*Fat Boy*
**Zinfandel**

**PREP TIME**
15 TO 20 MINUTES

**COOK TIME**
10 TO 12 MINUTES

**MAKES**
ONE 10 TO 12-INCH PIZZA

This pizza is a collection of the best, most flavorful ingredients you can pile on a pie. Built around linguica, a Portuguese cured sausage that's jam-packed with smoky flavor, this pizza is a Paso favorite—and Chef Marc's favorite, too! It is finished with briny peperoncini and the crisp bitterness of fresh arugula (or basil if you prefer). What's not to like about this pizza? Nothing. That's the answer. Absolutely nothing. In place of the pizza sauce, you can use the same amount of White Parmesan Sauce (page 183) or Marc's Basil Pesto Sauce (page 183).

One 10-oz ball pizza dough, homemade (page 178) or purchased

All-purpose flour, for dusting

½ cup pizza sauce, homemade (page 182) or purchased

2 cups shredded mozzarella cheese

½ cup thinly sliced linguica

½ cup sliced hot or mild peperoncini

½ cup sliced button mushrooms, in paper-thin slices

½ cup whole-milk ricotta cheese

1 or 2 large handfuls arugula, or fresh basil leaves (12 to 15 leaves)

**make the pizza**

Following the directions in Stretching the Dough & Baking the Pizza on page 180, prepare and preheat the oven to 550°F or higher, then prep the dough, dust the peel, stretch and bounce the dough until it is 10 to 12 inches in diameter, and transfer it to the peel. If you are using a store-bought crust, no worries! Just put it on the dusted peel.

Spread the entire pizza crust with the sauce, stopping within about ½ inch of the edge. Top the pizza evenly with the mozzarella, linguica, peperoncini, and mushrooms, making sure each slice will get an equal amount of each topping.

Using a spoon, add dollops of the ricotta, spacing them evenly over the top.

Slide the finished pizza onto the pizza stone (or overturned pan) and bake until the crust is a nice golden brown and the cheese is melted and bubbling, 10 to 12 minutes. Transfer the pizza to a cutting board. Wait for 3 to 5 minutes to allow the cheese to set slightly. Top with the arugula, slice, and enjoy! That's *amore!*

JUST ADD GREENS!

desserts

We're too full for dessert! Open another bottle of wine and maybe add some dark chocolate.

A PERFECT MATCH

side
dishes

The right accompaniment can make or break even the best entrée. Wow your guests with these one-of-a-kind side dishes and say goodbye to steamed vegetables.

# mashed potatoes

1 lb medium Yukon gold potatoes, peeled and halved

Kosher salt

½ cup cold unsalted butter, cut into ½-inch cubes

¼ cup crème fraîche or sour cream

In a medium saucepan, combine the potatoes with water to cover by about 2 inches and bring to a boil over high heat. Add 2 Tbsp salt, lower the heat to medium, and simmer until the potatoes are tender when pierced with a knife tip, 15 to 20 minutes.

Drain into a colander in the sink and let cool in the colander for 3 minutes. Pass the potatoes through a ricer back into the saucepan. If you don't have a ricer, use a stand mixer fitted with the paddle or whisk attachment and beat on medium speed until smooth, then return the potatoes to the saucepan.

Return the pan to medium heat and heat, stirring occasionally with a wooden spoon, until the potatoes are hot and steam starts to rise, about 2 minutes. The potatoes will start to stick to the bottom of the pan.

Add one-fourth of the butter cubes at a time, stirring constantly after each addition until fully incorporated before adding the next batch. When all of the butter has been incorporated, stir in the crème fraîche and season generously with salt. Serve right away.

**PREP TIME**
10 MINUTES

**COOK TIME**
20 TO 25 MINUTES

**MAKES**
4 SERVINGS

**GF/VEG**

# rosemary poppin' potatoes

1 lb baby (marble) potatoes, about 1 inch in diameter

1 Tbsp chopped fresh rosemary leaves

½ tsp chopped fresh thyme

4 garlic cloves, minced

2 Tbsp extra-virgin olive oil

Preheat the oven to 450°F.

In a medium bowl, toss the potatoes with the rosemary, thyme, garlic, and oil until evenly coated. Transfer to a sheet pan, spreading them in a single layer.

Roast until tender when pierced with a knife tip, about 30 minutes. That's it!

**CHEF PRO TIP:** The name for this side comes from the skins. When you roast a whole potato, the skin stays nice and firm, giving each bite a nice "pop" that's packed with herby goodness.

**PREP TIME**
5 MINUTES

**COOK TIME**
30 MINUTES

**MAKES**
4 SERVINGS

**GF/VEG/VG**

# cumin brown rice

1 Tbsp grapeseed oil

1 tsp cumin seeds

1 cup short-grain brown rice

2 cups chicken stock or vegetable stock, homemade (page 206) or purchased

1 tsp fine sea salt

½ tsp freshly ground black pepper

In a medium saucepan over medium-high heat, warm the oil. Add the cumin seeds and cook, stirring often, until fragrant, about 1 minute. Add the rice, stock, salt, and pepper, stir well, and bring to a simmer. Cover, turn down the heat to low, and cook until all the liquid is absorbed and the rice is tender, 40 to 50 minutes. Keep warm for serving.

**CHEF PRO TIP:** Cumin is a popular spice that brings a kick of freshness and flavor to your side dishes.

**PREP TIME**
5 MINUTES

**COOK TIME**
45 TO 55 MINUTES

**MAKES**
4 TO 6 SERVINGS

**GF/VEG/VG**

# cauliflower purée

1 head cauliflower, about 1 lb

½ cup raw cashews

8 garlic cloves

Kosher salt and ground white pepper

Remove any green leaves from the cauliflower head and discard. Cut the cauliflower, including the stem, into roughly 2-inch pieces and transfer them to a medium saucepan. Add the cashews, garlic, and water to cover by about 2 inches.

Bring everything to a boil over high heat. Turn down the heat to low and simmer until the cauliflower is tender, 8 to 10 minutes. You should be able to poke each piece easily with a fork or toothpick.

Drain the cauliflower mixture into a fine-mesh sieve placed over a heatproof bowl. Reserve the cooking water. Transfer the solids in the sieve to a high-speed blender. Turn on the blender to medium speed and slowly add just enough of the reserved cooking water for the blades to catch and spin. Be careful not to add too much water or the result will be too soupy! Blend until silky smooth, about 1 minute. The purée should look like thin mashed potatoes.

If needed, reheat the puree in the saucepan over low heat. Pour the purée into a bowl, season with salt and pepper, and serve it up.

**PREP TIME**
5 TO 10 MINUTES

**COOK TIME**
15 TO 20 MINUTES

**MAKES**
6 TO 8 SERVINGS

**GF/VEG/VG**

# "ancient grain" farro

1 cup farro, any kind

Kosher salt

1 Tbsp extra-virgin olive oil (optional; see **CHEF PRO TIP**)

Put the farro into a fine-mesh sieve and rinse under running cold water, swishing the farro around with your hand while rinsing to get it really clean. Drain off the excess water and transfer the farro to a medium saucepan.

Add 3 cups water and ¾ tsp salt to the saucepan and bring to a boil over high heat. Turn down the heat to a simmer, cover, and cook, stirring occasionally, for 25 minutes. If the water starts to boil over, turn down the heat slightly, give the farro a stir, and keep on going.

You can check for "doneness" by scooping out a few farro grains with a slotted spoon and tasting them. The farro should be tender yet chewy and not hard in the center—similar to al dente pasta. If the farro isn't ready, continue simmering, checking on it every 5 minutes. You may need to cook it for up to 20 minutes longer depending on the type of farro—whole grain, semi-pearled, or pearled—you are using. Add more water as needed.

When the farro is ready, drain it into a fine-mesh sieve and return it to the saucepan. Season to taste with salt (keep in mind you can always add more salt to the final preparation) and serve.

---

**CHEF PRO TIP:** If you're storing the cooked farro for later use, add the oil and stir to coat the grains to prevent them from sticking together.

---

**PREP TIME**
5 MINUTES

**COOK TIME**
35 TO 45 MINUTES

**MAKES**
4 TO 6 SERVINGS

**VEG/VG**

# salt-roasted beets

2 large beets, unpeeled, each about 3 inches in diameter

2 to 3 cups kosher salt

Preheat the oven to 400° F. Put the beets into a small baking pan and cover them completely with salt. The layer of salt on top of the beets must be at least ½ inch thick. Roast the beets until tender when pierced with a small paring knife, about 1 hour.

**CHEF PRO TIP:** The beets should be about the size of a baseball, as their size affects the cooking time. This recipe may seem like a colossal waste of salt, but it's not! You can reuse the salt multiple times for even tastier beets.

Remove from the oven and immediately pour the contents of the pan onto a sheet pan. Dust off the excess salt from the beets, then let the beets cool to room temperature.

Remove the skin from each beet. It should rub off easily with a paper towel. You can use a kitchen towel, but remember, this is a beet, so it's going to stain whatever towel you use! Once the salt cools, store it in an airtight container in a cupboard and reuse it for your next batch of beets.

The beets can be thinly sliced or cut into ¼-inch cubes, or each beet can be cut into six to eight wedges.

**PREP TIME**
10 TO 15 MINUTES

**COOK TIME**
1 HOUR

**MAKES**
4 SERVINGS

**GF/VEG/VG**

WINE AND BEETS ARE THE SAME COLOR... COINCIDENCE?

# stocks, sauces & more

The difference between a great meal and an unforgettable one is almost always the sauce. Take your dishes to the next level with any of these hand-crafted stocks, sauces, marmalades, and more. Be warned, some of these recipes aren't for the faint of heart, but if you persevere, these recipes will transform the way you cook.

# vegetable stock

2 celery stalks

2 large carrots

1 large yellow onion

4 to 6 green onions

1 Tbsp grapeseed oil

4 garlic cloves

8 fresh flat-leaf parsley sprigs

6 fresh thyme sprigs

2 bay leaves

Trim the celery, carrots, and yellow and green onions and cut into 1-inch chunks or lengths.

In a large stockpot over high heat, warm the oil until it begins to smoke lightly. Add all the cut vegetables along with the garlic, parsley, thyme, and bay leaves and cook, stirring frequently, until all the vegetables are soft, 5 to 10 minutes.

Pour in 8 cups water and bring to a boil. Turn down the heat to low and simmer, uncovered, for 30 minutes.

Strain the stock through a fine-mesh sieve and discard the solids. Use right away, or let cool, transfer to an airtight container, and store in the refrigerator for up to 7 days or in the freezer for up to 6 months.

**CHEF PRO TIP:** This stock can be made with other vegetables and herbs. Each kind you use will change the flavor profile. Mix and match vegetables and other ingredients as you like to discover your favorite flavor combination. Other good vegetable stock candidates include mushrooms, eggplant, asparagus (trimmed ends), corncobs, fennel (stalks and trimmings), bell peppers, pods from green peas, chard (stems and leaves), celery root parings, marjoram (stems and leaves), basil, potato peels—get the idea?

**PREP TIME**
20 MINUTES

**COOK TIME**
35 TO 40 MINUTES

**MAKES**
ABOUT 8 CUPS

**GF/VEG/VG**

# chicken stock

6 lb chicken parts (bones or a mix)

4 cups chopped yellow onions

2 cups chopped carrots

2 cups chopped celery

4 fresh flat-leaf parsley sprigs

16 black peppercorns

2 leeks, halved lengthwise and roughly chopped (optional)

6 garlic cloves, smashed (optional)

8 fresh thyme sprigs (optional)

4 bay leaves (optional)

Place the chicken bones and parts in an 8 qt stockpot and add the onions, carrots, celery, parsley, peppercorns, and the leek, garlic, thyme, and bay leaves, if using. Pour in 4 qt water and bring to a simmer over medium heat. Do not allow the water to boil. You want there to be movement and some bubbles around the edges but not a rolling boil. Boiling will turn the stock cloudy. You want a clear liquid.

Once you have a nice simmer going, cook the stock uncovered for 2 hours, occasionally skimming off any foam that rises to the top. After 2 hours, check the stock to see if it has enough flavor. If it doesn't, simmer for another 30 minutes.

Remove from the heat and scoop out and discard the chicken and the leek, if using. Strain the stock through a fine-mesh sieve into a heatproof bowl and discard the remaining solids. You should have a clear, yellow stock.

Use a fat separator to skim off the fat, or let the stock cool, cover, and refrigerate until the fat has solidified on the surface, at least 2 hours, and then lift off and discard the fat. The stock will keep in a covered container in the refrigerator for 7 days or in the freezer for up to 6 months.

**PREP TIME**
20 MINUTES

**COOK TIME**
2 TO 2½ HOURS

**MAKES**
ABOUT 8 CUPS

**GF**

# rich veal or beef stock

5 lb assorted veal or beef bones, such as knuckle and leg bones, cut into 3-inch pieces by the butcher

2 medium carrots, roughly chopped

3 medium yellow onions, roughly chopped

2 celery stalks, roughly chopped

1 leek, white and green parts, roughly chopped

**BOUQUET GARNI**

2 cups chopped fresh flat-leaf parsley, leaves and tender stems

2 Tbsp black peppercorns

3 bay leaves

## roast the bones and vegetables

Preheat the oven to 350°F. Spread the bones in a single layer on a sheet pan. The rim of the pan keeps the grease from spilling over into the oven. Roast for 30 minutes. After 30 minutes, turn the bones over and lay the carrot, onion, celery, and leek on top of the bones. Roast, tossing the mix several times during the process, until the vegetables and bones have begun to take on a nice color, about 30 minutes.

## make the bouquet garni

Put the parsley, peppercorns, and bay leaves on a 12-inch square of cheesecloth, bring the cheesecloth corners together, and tie the bundle closed with kitchen twine.

## make the stock

Transfer the roasted vegetables and bones to a large stockpot, discarding any extra fatty oil from the bones. The pot must be large enough so that once the liquid is added, the pot is only three-quarters full. Add 2 gallons water and the bouquet garni and bring to a boil over high heat. Turn down the heat to low and simmer gently, uncovered, occasionally skimming off any foam that rises to the top, until the liquid reduces to about 8 cups. This will take 6 to 8 hours.

Remove from the heat and scoop out and discard the bones and bouquet garni. Strain the stock through a fine-mesh sieve set over a large, heatproof bowl and discard the remaining solids. Use a fat separator to skim off the fat, or let the stock cool, cover, and refrigerate until the fat has solidified on the surface, at least 2 hours, and then lift off and discard the fat.

When this is done, you will have your stock. It will keep in an airtight container in the refrigerator for up to 7 days or in the freezer for up to 6 months.

**PREP TIME**
10 TO 20 MINUTES

**COOK TIME**
7 TO 9 HOURS

**MAKES**
8 CUPS

GF

*GO BIG!*

# veal or beef demi-glace

Canola oil in a kitchen-oil spritzer (see **CHEF PRO TIP**)

¼ cup finely chopped shallot (about 1 large shallot)

2 garlic cloves, finely chopped

¼ cup red wine

2 cups veal or beef stock, homemade (page 207) or purchased

Kosher salt and freshly ground black pepper

1 Tbsp cornstarch

Spritz a medium saucepan with canola oil and warm over medium heat.

---

**CHEF PRO TIP:** At the winery kitchen, we put high-quality cooking oils in a kitchen-oil spritzer rather than buying in aerosol cans.

---

Add shallot and garlic and cook, stirring occasionally, until the shallot is translucent, about 5 minutes. Add red wine to deglaze the saucepan and simmer, stirring and scraping up browned bits from the bottom of the pan, until the liquid has almost evaporated, about 4 minutes.

Add the stock and ¾ cup water, raise the heat to medium-high, and bring to a boil. Lower the heat to medium and simmer until the mixture has reduced to 2 cups, about 5 minutes. Season to taste with the salt and pepper.

In a small bowl, stir together the cornstarch and 1 Tbsp water to form a paste. Stir the paste into the demi-glace and continue to simmer over medium heat until thickened, about 1 more minute. Remove from the heat, let cool, and use as directed in individual recipes, or transfer to an airtight container and refrigerate for up to 7 days or freeze for up to 6 months.

**recipes**

**coffee-rubbed filet mignon (page 169)**

**bacon pork tenderloin "roulade" (page 152)**

| PREP TIME |
|---|
| 5 MINUTES |
| **COOK TIME** |
| 15 TO 20 MINUTES |
| **MAKES** |
| 2 CUPS |
| **GF** |

# tartar sauce

1 cup mayonnaise

¼ cup dill pickle relish

1 Tbsp drained capers, chopped

2 dashes of Tabasco sauce

2 dashes of Worcestershire sauce

1 tsp fresh lemon juice

Kosher salt and freshly ground black pepper

In a medium stainless-steel or glass bowl, whisk together the mayonnaise, pickle relish, capers, Tabasco sauce, Worcestershire sauce, and lemon juice until thoroughly blended. Season with salt and pepper and whisk again. Cover and refrigerate for at least 10 to 15 minutes before serving. It will keep for up to 5 to 7 days.

**recipe**

**dungeness crab cakes (page 42)**

| PREP TIME |
|---|
| 5 MINUTES |
| **MAKES** |
| ABOUT 1½ CUPS |
| **GF** |

# bacon-onion marmalade

1 Tbsp grapeseed oil

6 slices hickory-smoked bacon, cut into ¼-inch dice

1 cup diced red onion

2 cups *Ballistic* Zinfandel wine

½ cup firmly packed dark brown sugar

In a medium frying pan over medium-high heat, combine the grapeseed oil and bacon and cook, stirring occasionally, until the bacon is crispy and all the fat has rendered out. This will take 5 to 10 minutes, depending on how fatty the bacon is. Using a slotted spoon, transfer the bacon to a plate lined with paper towels. Leave the fat in the pan.

Lower the heat to medium, add the onion, and cook, stirring occasionally, until golden brown and delicious, about 5 minutes.

Drain off the excess fat from the pan, then return the pan to low heat. Add the wine and deglaze the pan, stirring to scrape up the browned bits from the bottom. Simmer, uncovered, until the wine thickens and reduces to 1 cup. This will take 15 to 20 minutes.

Once the wine has reduced, stir in the sugar until it dissolves and then continue to simmer over low heat for 1 minute. Fold in the cooked bacon, remove the pan from the heat, and let cool. When the mixture has cooled, it should look like jam with bacon bits in it. Use right away, or transfer to an airtight container and store in the refrigerator for up to 7 days or freeze for up to 6 months.

**recipes**
**brie crostini with bacon-onion marmalade (page 45)**

**"slow jams" zinfandel jam burger (page 170)**

| | |
|---|---|
| **PREP TIME** | 10 MINUTES |
| **COOK TIME** | 30 TO 40 MINUTES |
| **MAKES** | ABOUT 1 CUP |
| GF | |

# cilantro-mint chutney

2 cups firmly packed fresh cilantro leaves and coarsely chopped stems

1 cup firmly packed fresh mint leaves

2 garlic cloves, minced

1½ teaspoons diced jalapeño chile

2 Tbsp fresh lemon juice

2 tsp cumin seeds, ground

1 tsp kosher salt

In a blender, combine all the ingredients with ¾ cup water and blend until smooth, about 1 minute. The chutney is best if served right away, though in a pinch, it will keep in an airtight container in the refrigerator for 3 days.

**CHEF PRO TIP:** Mincing the garlic, dicing the jalapeño, and grinding the cumin seeds before they go in the blender will help the blender mix everything together more smoothly for a better end result.

**recipe**
**roasted chicken tikka masala (page 151)**

| | |
|---|---|
| **PREP TIME** | 5 TO 10 MINUTES |
| **MAKES** | 4 SERVINGS |
| GF/VEG/VG | |

# besciamella with parmesan cheese sauce

2 cups whole milk

3 Tbsp unsalted butter

¼ cup sifted all-purpose flour

Kosher salt and freshly ground black pepper

1 cup grated Parmesan cheese

Pour the milk into a medium saucepan and heat over medium until just below boiling. While the milk is heating, in a medium, heavy saucepan over medium-low heat, melt the butter. Add flour and whisk for 1½ minutes. Don't allow it to burn!

Gradually add the hot milk to the butter mixture while whisking constantly. Season with salt and pepper and continue to cook, stirring constantly with a wooden spoon, until the sauce is thick and smooth, about 15 minutes. Finally, add the Parmesan and cook, stirring, until the cheese is melted and the sauce is smooth, about 1 minute.

The sauce should be thick and creamy and friggin' delicious. It goes great with "Not Your Average" Lasagna (page 174).

**recipes**

**"not your average" lasagna (page 174)**

**"the colossus" wild mushroom ravioli (page 117)**

| | |
|---|---|
| **PREP TIME** | 5 MINUTES |
| **COOK TIME** | 20 MINUTES |
| **MAKES** | ABOUT 2 CUPS; 6 TO 8 SERVINGS |
| **VEG** | |

# chef marc's marinara sauce

¼ cup extra-virgin olive oil

3 garlic cloves, halved

1 Tbsp tomato paste

One 28-oz can whole San Marzano tomatoes with juices

½ tsp sugar or honey

1 cup loosely packed fresh basil leaves

Kosher salt and freshly ground black pepper

In a large saucepan over medium heat, warm the oil. Once the oil has started to heat up, after about 1 minute, add the garlic and cook, stirring occasionally, until golden brown, about 3 minutes. Add the tomato paste and cook, stirring, for 1 more minute.

Add the tomatoes and use a wooden spoon to crush them into pieces. The size of the pieces depends on how chunky you want your marinara sauce. Stir in the sugar and basil leaves and then season with salt and pepper.

Turn down the heat to medium-low and simmer until the sauce is reduced to about 3 cups,

about 25 minutes. Cooking the sauce slowly helps the flavors blend, and it won't bubble and splatter everywhere, which is great.

Remove from the heat and use right away, or let cool and store in an airtight container in the refrigerator for up to 7 days or in the freezer for up to 6 months.

**recipe**

**"not your average" lasagna (page 174)**

| | |
|---|---|
| **PREP TIME** | 5 TO 10 MINUTES |
| **COOK TIME** | 30 MINUTES |
| **MAKES** | ABOUT 3 CUPS; 4 SERVINGS |
| **GF/VEG/VG** | |

# sesame-mustard sauce

2 Tbsp soy sauce or tamari

1 Tbsp molasses

1 Tbsp honey

1 Tbsp sesame seeds

1½ tsp cornstarch

1 tsp minced peeled fresh ginger

1 tsp minced garlic

1 tsp mustard powder

¼ tsp freshly ground black pepper

In a small saucepan, stir together all the ingredients with ¾ cup water and bring to a simmer over medium-high heat while whisking constantly. Cook, whisking constantly, until nicely thickened, about 5 minutes. Remove from the heat and keep warm until it's time to serve.

**recipe**

**miso-marinated sea bass with sesame-mustard sauce (page 133)**

**PREP TIME**
5 TO 10 MINUTES

**COOK TIME**
5 MINUTES

**MAKES**
ABOUT 1 CUP;
4 SERVINGS

**GF/VEG**

# pickled red onions

1 large red onion

1 cup hot or warm water

½ cup apple cider vinegar

1 Tbsp sugar

1½ tsp kosher salt

Slice the red onion as thinly as you can. A mandoline works great. Stuff the red onion slices into a wide-mouthed jar of your choice. A bowl will work, too.

In a measuring cup, combine the hot water, vinegar, sugar, and salt and stir to dissolve the sugar and salt. Pour this pickling mixture over the onion slices, making sure they are immersed in the liquid, and let them sit for 1 hour.

After 1 hour, the onions are ready to eat, but you can also cover and store them in the fridge for up to 3 weeks.

**recipes**

**sea salt–massaged kale salad (page 55)**

**greek salad bites (page 67)**

**the "wine wednesday" wedge (page 71)**

**PREP TIME**
10 TO 15 MINUTES

**MAKES**
1 TO 1½ CUPS

**GF/VEG**

# the team

## Marc LeDuc
### Executive Chef, Tobin James Cellars

Marc LeDuc's passion for the culinary world was sparked at age six while watching his renowned professional chef uncle work in the kitchen. By age fourteen, it was no surprise to anyone who knew him that Chef Marc had already begun his restaurant career, working at a popular, family-run Italian restaurant.

A native of Chicago, Illinois, Chef Marc enrolled in Johnson & Wales University in Charleston, South Carolina, earning a degree in culinary arts. And if that weren't enough, during his four-year university education, he won gold and silver medals as a member of the US Junior Olympic Culinary Team.

Determined to expand his culinary knowledge following graduation, Chef Marc went to stage (intern) with some of America's top chefs, including Thomas Keller, Norman Van Aken, and Kevin Montoya. It was during these internships that he began to explore his love of regional cuisine and modern cooking techniques, and as his culinary experiences grew, he began establishing his own unique style.

In 1997, Chef Marc was hired by Priscilla and Lisa Marie Presley as the opening chef for Elvis Presley's Memphis, located on Beale Street. Later, he moved to the Caribbean to learn about its regional cuisines. Soon after, he became the sous chef at Asolare, on the Island of St. John in the Virgin Islands. During his time there, Asolare was one of the islands' top restaurants, featured in many magazines articles and on television travel shows.

After his stay in the Caribbean, Chef Marc relocated to Steamboat Springs, in the Rocky Mountains of Colorado. He became the banquet chef for the Steamboat Grand, a luxurious, four-star mountain ski resort. Chef Marc later accepted the executive chef position at The Lodge and Spa at Three Forks Ranch, about forty miles north of Steamboat Springs. He went on to design and develop the brand-new venue's hotel restaurants and kitchens. It was at Three Forks that he gained national acclaim as the executive chef at one of the top boutique hotels in the United States. His accomplishments were featured in *Bon Appétit*, *Travel & Leisure*, and *Wine Spectator*, among other publications. Most important to Chef Marc, it was in Colorado that he developed his own style of high-country comfort food based on farm-to-table and sustainable food sources.

In 2011, Chef Marc moved to Paso Robles wine country, on California's Central Coast, where he accepted the position of executive chef at Tobin James Cellars. Here, he is expanding his passions for fine food and wine, focusing on locally produced organic products and Tobin James food and wine pairings.

He enjoys sharing his culinary gifts with members of the popular "James Gang," and they enjoy receiving them! He's immensely proud to present you with these handcrafted recipes designed specifically for Tobin James wines.

## Lance Silver
**Co-owner/Co-winemaker,**
**Tobin James Cellars**

Lance Silver's love for wine began early. At age seventeen, he started collecting wine with money made from mowing lawns. At the University of Nevada, Las Vegas he took courses in the sensory evaluation of wine, wine tasting, and wine education. In 1996, Lance and his wife, Claire, became co-owners and equal partners of Tobin James Cellars, allowing him to finally follow his long-held passion. Lance's proudest accomplishment at Tobin James Cellars is that the winery has grown twenty times over in the past thirty-five years, and each wine is better than ever.

## Claire Silver
**Co-owner/Co-winemaker,**
**Tobin James Cellars**

Claire Silver grew up in a family that enjoyed wine with dinner. She met Lance at the University of Nevada, Las Vegas, where they were both in the hotel administration program. A wine course and meeting Lance opened the door to a whole new level of wine appreciation for Claire. For seven years, she served as acting president of the Wineries of Highway 46 East, an association of wineries and lodgings in Paso Robles. She has also been a member of the advisory board of both the Paso Robles Culinary School and the Endeavour Academy. Claire's main interests and true passions are her family and Tobin James Cellars. She is especially proud of Lance, her husband of forty years, and their two grown daughters.

## Tobin James
**Co-owner/Co-winemaker,**
**Tobin James Cellars**

Tobin "Toby" James was raised in Cincinnati, Ohio, where he spent every summer of his youth working on his family's vineyard just across the border in Indiana. At nineteen years old, he bought a one-way ticket to California and began his career in wine as a "cellar rat," eventually working his way up to winemaker for several of Paso Robles' most notable wineries. In 1993, Toby purchased forty-one acres at the end of Union Road in Paso Robles, where he built Tobin James Cellars. A year later, the winery and tasting room opened. Toby's greatest passion is his family—his wife, Ermie, and their four children.

## Shawn Forno
**Author**

Shawn Forno is a very left-handed travel writer and native Californian who writes for the internet. He volunteered to write this cookbook with his then-girlfriend and now-wife, Elaine, and his in-laws in large part because he's a huge fan of Chef Marc's cauliflower purée (seriously, it's ridiculous). This is his first cookbook.

## Elaine Silver
**Producer, Photographer, and Editor**

Elaine Silver grew up at Tobin James Cellars. After spending thirteen years in New York City as a professional dancer, Elaine returned to her roots in Paso Robles. She's loved working with her mom and dad, Claire and Lance, making their dreams of this cookbook come true. She's a Lindy Hop dancer and teacher; runs a YouTube travel channel with her husband, Shawn; and is the social media manager of Tobin James Cellars.

## Kate Voegele
**Cover Artist**

Kate Voegele is a California-based creative, singer-songwriter, and actress. A longtime James Gang member, Kate has created much of her art and music with the aid of a glass of Tobin James wine. She has spent the past decade releasing four studio albums, racking up millions of streams, accumulating a global fan base, and touring all over the world with her music and art. Her acting career includes a four-season run on the hit television show *One Tree Hill*. Kate currently lives in Los Angeles, where she spends her days painting in her studio; writing for her blog, *We The Dreamers*; writing songs; and producing music for herself and others.

## Christopher N. Gallegos
**Interior Sketch Artist**

Christopher N. Gallegos is an architectural designer who trained on the East Coast and is currently living and working on the West Coast. He found his soul mate, Melanie, daughter of Claire and Lance Silver, and they have been happily married for more than four years. In his free time, he loves hiking in strange locales, analyzing how things go together, sampling regional wines, and sketching both man-made and natural environments.

# acknowledgments (the thanks)

Deepest gratitude and heartfelt thanks to all our family, friends, and the Tobin James Cellars staff for their help and hard work creating this precious book.

Our biggest thank you to Shawn Forno and Elaine Silver. Without you, this book would not have been possible. Shawn spent hours writing recipes with Chef Marc, researching publishers, and learning the language of cookbooks. Elaine kept everyone on track with deadlines, collaborated with Chef Marc on food styling, shot and reshot almost all the photographs in this book, and was so instrumental in the design and communication with our publishers.

Chef Marc, your inspirational work ethic, incredible talent in the kitchen, and endless patience are the foundations of this book. There are not enough words to express our appreciation. Thank you for over a decade of friendship, amazing food, and lots of laughter. We hope we get a five-star review in the LeDuc Chronicles.

This cookbook—and Tobin James Cellars—only exists because of our caring, outstanding, and dedicated staff. Thank you for being an integral part of our vision to make the best wines possible, and for putting us on the map as the most welcoming winery in Paso Robles. This book became a reality because of the decades of phenomenal wines you have produced and put into glasses for so many to enjoy. A huge thank you is not enough to express how we feel toward our outstanding staff. An extra-special mention to our twenty-five-plus-year General Manager Monica Martin. Special mention to our twenty-plus-years team members: Erica Fletcher, Tim Martin, Karla Murray, Jorge Mercado, Ben Lunt, Jeff Poe, and Bob Zavala. Fifteen-plus-years team members: Pam, Cheyenne, Holly, Shawna, Chili, Amanda D, and Terrie. Ten-plus-years team members: Gaetano, Roy, Kaye, Charleen, Bethany, Chef Marc, David Z, Jill J, Karina, Ione, Amanda K, and Cesar. To the rest of our dedicated team members on the way to their ten-year anniversaries, we appreciate all of you so very much.

We couldn't have made this cookbook without our incredible and patient recipe testers: Charleen Borla, Richard Coffey, Lance and Sandy Cutler, Erin Delaney, Amanda Dominguez, Pam Estrada, Heather Evers, Erica Fletcher, Bethany Grimes, Ione Harrington, Sara Irwin, Jill Jones, Shawna Kamber, Amanda Keith, Ben Lunt, Gaetano Marsano, Monica Martin, Eileen Morones, Ermie Morones, Sheila Morrissey and Randy Whitney, Kelly Munns, Karla Murray, Holly Olcott, Chris Pascone, Terri Perkiss, Nicole Piccetti, Melanie Silver and Christopher Gallegos, Tatiana Smeltzer, and Stefanie Tringham.

Our incredible team at Chronicle Books gave life to this book. Pamela Geismar for the expert art direction, layout, and thoughtful design (and patience for all our changes!). Danielle Youngsmith for giving this book color and life with your designs. Kim Laidlaw for her keen editorial eye. Catherine Huchting and Beth Weber for connecting us with the amazing Chronicle team.

We also want to thank our artists, Kate Voegele and Christopher Gallegos. Kate, your gorgeous painting on our cover absolutely makes the book. Chris, your original and intricate drawings for our book are a treasured gift. Thank you to Melanie Silver for your creative eye and graphic assistance.

Tobin James Cellars newest iconic wine is **"the blend."** The name was the inspiration for the title and the features in this book. Open a bottle of **"the blend"** and you'll understand why.

Finally, we want to thank each and every one of our loyal James Gang wine club members. Without you, this cookbook (or the winery!) simply wouldn't exist. You've been the core of our winery for the past thirty-five years, and we look forward to many more years sharing stories over a bottle (or two) at Tobin James Cellars.

Cheers!
Lance and Claire Silver

CHEERS!

# wine pairing index

## white wines

### Chardonnay *James Gang Reserve*

| | |
|---|---|
| "one & only" shrimp cocktail | 38 |
| dungeness crab cakes | 42 |
| "char-donnay" grilled romaine salad | 64 |
| the "wine wednesday" wedge | 71 |
| james gang tuscan white bean soup | 82 |
| provençal lentil soup | 88 |
| quinoa & hearts of palm cakes | 107 |
| brown butter pasta with ricotta salata | 108 |
| bella bella black pepper fettuccine | 114 |
| petrale sole in parchment | 128 |
| brick chicken | 143 |
| leduc's lemon roasted chicken | 144 |
| bone-in double pork chop | 156 |
| pear & gorgonzola pizza | 186 |

### Chardonnay *Radiance*

| | |
|---|---|
| watermelon, feta, basil & chili bites | 27 |
| kale, caesar! | 68 |
| shiitake "bacon" lettuce cups | 73 |
| madras curry carrot soup | 81 |
| quinoa & hearts of palm cakes | 107 |
| pacific snapper with fresh peach salsa | 124 |
| miso-marinated sea bass with sesame-mustard sauce | 133 |
| cast-iron diver sea scallops | 137 |
| the big dill pickle pizza | 189 |
| too much garlic & shrimp pizza | 190 |

### Riesling *James Gang Reserve*

| | |
|---|---|
| melon & arugula salad | 56 |
| shiitake "bacon" lettuce cups | 73 |
| chilled pea & mint soup | 78 |
| madras curry carrot soup | 81 |
| green lentil & veggie curry | 119 |
| too much garlic & shrimp pizza | 190 |

### Sauvignon Blanc *Sundance*

| | |
|---|---|
| fig, serrano ham & goat cheese bites | 32 |
| bbq oysters with spicy tarragon butter | 35 |
| "one & only" shrimp cocktail | 38 |
| sea salt–massaged kale salad | 55 |
| melon & arugula salad | 56 |
| salt-roasted beet & arugula salad | 63 |
| greek salad bites | 67 |
| kale, caesar! | 68 |
| california heirloom tomato gazpacho | 76 |
| mustard-crusted black cod | 127 |
| petrale sole in parchment | 128 |
| *TnT* grilled smoky shrimp | 138 |
| roasted chicken tikka masala | 151 |

### Sparkling *Dream Weaver*

| | |
|---|---|
| watermelon, feta, basil & chili bites | 27 |
| bbq oysters with spicy tarragon butter | 35 |
| ahi tuna poke | 41 |
| green lentil & veggie curry | 119 |
| roasted chicken tikka masala | 151 |

## rosé wines

### Rosé *Paradise*

| | |
|---|---|
| fig, serrano ham & goat cheese bites | 32 |
| "one & only" shrimp cocktail | 38 |
| dungeness crab cakes | 42 |
| french bibb lettuce & herbs | 52 |
| greek salad bites | 67 |
| quinoa & hearts of palm cakes | 107 |

## red wine blends

**5 Bordeaux Style Blend**

| | |
|---|---|
| rack of lamb with mint *pistou* | 159 |
| coffee-rubbed filet mignon | 169 |
| cruisin' braised beef short ribs | 173 |

**Big Shot Rhone Style Blend**

| | |
|---|---|
| wild mushroom tartlets | 31 |

**Chateau Le Cacheflo**

| | |
|---|---|
| *primo* minestrone | 92 |
| beef & barley harvest soup | 100 |
| brown butter pasta with ricotta salata | 108 |
| leduc's lemon roasted chicken | 144 |
| rack of lamb with mint *pistou* | 159 |
| the big dill pickle pizza | 189 |

**GSM Blend**

| | |
|---|---|
| provençal lentil soup | 88 |
| red wine–braised chicken | 147 |
| bacon pork tenderloin "roulade" | 152 |
| *rock-n-roll* syrah braised lamb shank | 160 |

**Private Stash**

| | |
|---|---|
| beef & barley harvest soup | 100 |
| grilled ny strip with smoked onion butter | 166 |

**RED Blend**

| | |
|---|---|
| california heirloom tomato gazpacho | 76 |
| cedar plank salmon with red wine sauce | 134 |

**Schist Portuguese Blend**

| | |
|---|---|
| grilled ny strip with smoked onion butter | 166 |
| cruisin' braised beef short ribs | 173 |

**the blend**

| | |
|---|---|
| "slow jams" zinfandel jam burger | 170 |

**TNT Tannat/Tempranillo Blend**

| | |
|---|---|
| *TNT* grilled smoky shrimp | 138 |

## red wines

**Barbera Bella Bella**

| | |
|---|---|
| bella bella black pepper fettuccine | 114 |
| red wine risotto | 120 |

**Cabernet Franc James Gang Reserve**

| | |
|---|---|
| wild mushroom tartlet | 31 |

**Cabernet Sauvignon Blue Moon Reserve**

| | |
|---|---|
| coffee-rubbed filet mignon | 169 |
| cruisin' braised beef short ribs | 173 |

**Cabernet Sauvignon James Gang Reserve**

| | |
|---|---|
| coffee-rubbed filet mignon | 169 |

**Cabernet Sauvignon Notorious**

| | |
|---|---|
| low 'n' slow tri-tip with red wine aioli | 46 |
| *notorious* cuban black bean soup | 99 |
| leduc's lemon roasted chicken | 144 |
| cruisin' braised beef short ribs | 173 |

**Lagrein Silver Reserve**

| | |
|---|---|
| red wine risotto | 120 |

**Merlot Made in the Shade**

| | |
|---|---|
| red wine–braised chicken | 147 |

**Merlot Silver Reserve**

| | |
|---|---|
| brick chicken | 143 |

DRY-FARMED DUSI VINEYARD ZINFANDEL

## Nebbiolo *Pasorolo*

| | |
|---|---|
| james gang tuscan white bean soup | 82 |
| *primo* minestrone | 92 |
| beef & barley harvest soup | 100 |
| "the colossus" wild mushroom ravioli | 117 |
| "not your average" lasagna | 175 |

## Petite Sirah *Midnight Magic*

| | |
|---|---|
| bone-in double pork chop | 156 |

## Petite Sirah *Silver Reserve*

| | |
|---|---|
| bone-in double pork chop | 156 |
| rack of lamb with mint *pistou* | 159 |

## Petit Verdot *James Gang Reserve*

| | |
|---|---|
| low 'n' slow tri-tip with red wine aioli | 46 |

## Pinot Noir *Tobin James*

| | |
|---|---|
| mustard-crusted black cod | 127 |
| cedar plank salmon with red wine sauce | 134 |
| T𝘯T grilled smoky shrimp | 138 |
| red wine–braised chicken | 147 |

## Primitivo *James Gang Reserve*

| | |
|---|---|
| italian wine & wedding soup | 91 |
| *primo* minestrone | 92 |
| leduc's lemon roasted chicken | 144 |

## Sangiovese *Primo*

| | |
|---|---|
| sea salt–massaged kale salad | 55 |
| james gang tuscan white bean soup | 82 |
| fat fungi mushroom soup | 87 |
| *primo* minestrone | 92 |
| brown butter pasta with ricotta salata | 108 |
| red wine risotto | 120 |
| cedar plank salmon with red wine sauce | 134 |

## Syrah *Blue Moon Reserve*

| | |
|---|---|
| smoky walnut & brie crostini | 28 |

## Syrah *James Gang Reserve*

| | |
|---|---|
| grilled ny strip with smoked onion butter | 166 |

## Syrah *Rock-N-Roll*

| | |
|---|---|
| *rock-n-roll* syrah braised lamb shank | 160 |

## Tannat *Palindrome*

| | |
|---|---|
| low 'n' slow tri-tip with red wine aioli | 46 |
| grilled ny strip with smoked onion butter | 166 |

## Zinfandel *Ballistic*

| | |
|---|---|
| brie crostini with bacon-onion marmalade | 45 |
| the "wine wednesday" wedge | 71 |
| italian wine & wedding soup | 91 |
| *ballistic* flank steak chili | 103 |
| miso-marinated sea bass with sesame-mustard sauce | 133 |
| "slow jams" zinfandel jam burger | 170 |
| chef's favorite sausage & mushroom pizza with peperoncini | 193 |

## Zinfandel *Dusi Vineyard*

| | |
|---|---|
| bacon pork tenderloin "roulade" | 152 |
| the big deal bolognese pasta | 165 |

## Zinfandel *Fat Boy*

| | |
|---|---|
| fat fungi mushroom soup | 87 |
| bacon pork tenderloin "roulade" | 152 |
| "slow jams" zinfandel jam burger | 170 |
| "not your average" lasagna | 175 |
| chef's favorite sausage & mushroom pizza with peperoncini | 193 |

## Zinfandel *French Camp Vineyard*

| | |
|---|---|
| brie crostini with bacon-onion marmalade | 45 |
| pear & gorgonzola pizza | 186 |

## Zinfandel *James Gang Reserve*

| | |
|---|---|
| brie crostini with bacon-onion marmalade | 45 |
| winemaker's chicken tortilla soup | 96 |
| the big deal bolognese pasta | 165 |

## Zinfandel *Silver Reserve*

| | |
|---|---|
| "the colossus" wild mushroom ravioli | 117 |
| bone-in double pork chop | 156 |

# index

Claire and Lance Silver enjoy a barrel sampling.